Lent of Liberation

Find digital resources for study and preaching
at www.wjkbooks.com/LentOfLiberation.

Lent of Liberation

Confronting the Legacy of American Slavery

CHERI L. MILLS

WESTMINSTER
JOHN KNOX PRESS
LOUISVILLE • KENTUCKY

First edition
Published by Westminster John Knox Press
Louisville, Kentucky

21 22 23 24 25 26 27 28 29 30—10 9 8 7 6 5 4 3 2 1

Book design by Drew Stevens
Cover design by Marc Whitaker / MTWdesign.net
Cover illustration: Slave in Chains, *portrait painting, c. 1820 / incamerastock / Alamy Stock Photo*

Library of Congress Cataloging-in-Publication Data is on file at the Library of Congress, Washington, DC.

ISBN-13: 978-0-664-26683-7

I write this book with the hopes that the martyrdom of Ahmaud Arbery, Breonna Taylor, and George Floyd will not be in vain — that justice may one day come to the American Descendants of Slavery.

Contents

Introduction

In 1619, forcibly captured Africans arrived in colonial America for the purpose of providing a free labor force to the expanding British territories in the Americas. The year 2019 marked 400 years since the institution of Slavery began with the first "20 and odd Negroes" who were brought to the British colonies.[1] This institution was sustained until the passage of the Thirteenth Amendment. However, as lawyer and social justice activist Bryan Stevenson asserts, "Slavery didn't end in 1865; it just evolved."[2]

Throughout these 400 years—starting with those enslaved in America and then with the American Descendants of Slavery—Black people have experienced a Black Holocaust: enslavement, black codes, sharecropping, Jim Crow, lynchings, convict leasing, redlining, restrictive covenants, police brutality, subprime lending, and mass incarceration, all of which have resulted in the ghettoization/impoverishment of Black communities across America.

Dr. Martin Luther King Jr. asserted that because Blacks were targeted for special mistreatment, then Blacks should be targeted for special treatment.[3] Blacks who are American Descendants of Slavery can trace their lineage back to American Slavery and the Jim Crow era. This is the specific group that has historically been made to eat the cost for the success of American capitalism. With that, the recent arrival of Black immigrants to the United States who voluntarily came to the U.S. from other countries would not be included in the American Descendants of Slavery category as their lineage is in another country, and so their justice claim, as it pertains to reparations, would be with the country that enslaved and oppressed their ancestors, and not with the United States.

Four hundred and one years after the institution of Slavery began in 1619, in the year 2020, the world witnessed the blatant disregard for Black life in America, which was on full display for the world to see. People around the globe saw the brutality of a Minneapolis police officer and three fellow officers in the horrific murder of George Floyd that was streamed live. For eight minutes and forty-six seconds, as George lay facedown on the pavement with his hands handcuffed behind his back, one policeman knelt with his knee pressed against George's neck, restricting his airflow. The other two policemen compressed his abdomen and legs, which restricted blood and airflow, as he pleaded for his life. The fourth officer stood watch and attempted to block the view of this criminal act. George cried out numerous times, "I can't breathe, I can't breathe, I can't breathe!" Realizing he was about to die, he cried out for his momma. As the world watched in horror, George took his last breath and his body went limp.

The world finally saw the targeted abuse that the masses of Black people in America have been asserting for years. Then, an unprecedented eruption took place—there was civil unrest, with protests and marches in every state in America that quickly spread to other countries around the globe. At the writing of this book, the protests are still growing.

It is at this precipice that we invite Blacks, Whites, and people across racial, denominational, faith, and cultural lines to participate in a Lent of Liberation. Lent is a time for personal reflection as we march toward Good Friday and Resurrection Sunday. The forty days of Lent are to remind us of the forty days Jesus spent in the wilderness, fasting and praying, practicing self-denial to commit himself fully to the will of God. This time was a prelude to his great Galilean ministry, in which he would say "If any want to become my followers, let them deny themselves and take up their cross and follow me" (Matt. 16:24). Even as the community is erupting in protests, there are still those who push back because White supremacy is so ingrained in our nation's DNA. Lent is a time of denial, but not denial of the truth—the spirit of Lent must lead us to confront the legacy of American Slavery head-on if we are to overcome the centuries of White privilege at Black expense.

Included in each daily devotion is an excerpt from the documentary book *The Underground Railroad: A Record* by William Still.[4] William escaped from the bondage of Slavery as a child along with his mother. As an adult, he committed his life to assisting Black bondservants to freedom through the Underground Railroad in the 1800s. It is estimated that William assisted over 800 slaves in their quest for freedom and he documented the testimony of those he assisted. As a result of William's documentation, the reader hears up close and personal the testimony of the slaves who escaped on the Underground Railroad, which showcases their humanity. They were people, not property—they were someone's husband, wife, sister, brother, grandmother and grandfather.

This devotional also imparts little-known facts about how the institution of Slavery actually built America, and how ongoing oppression has affected Black Americans. Since Black history is not usually taught as a part of American history in the U.S. school system, more false narratives are circulated about Slavery than fact. In the words of Yvette Carnell, cofounder of #ADOS (American Descendents of Slavery, a grass-roots reparation movement), "There can be no peace without justice, but there can be no justice without truth." Through scriptural reflection and questions to ponder at the end of each daily devotion, this devotional prompts the reader to move from compassion to action for the cause of racial justice and to reflect upon ways that they may have contributed to racial injustices. These questions may appear to be tailored to only White people; however, this book is written with the belief that the White supremacist view is an ideology—it is not based on skin color and certainly not based on fact. Thus, many ethnic groups in America adopt the White supremacist views to assimilate into the dominant culture, and can be agents of White supremacy—even some Blacks! Na'im Akbar, noted scholar and psychologist, espouses that some Blacks have an anti-self disorder whereby they see themselves through the lens of White supremacy. With the slave rebellions that occurred prior to the abolishment of Slavery, each rebellion was sabotaged by a Black enslaved person who served as an informant. Consequently, all skin folk ain't your kin folk! A misnomer is that the White supremacist is the person who advocates violence against Blacks or promotes hateful, racist language. That's too simplistic a definition— White supremacy involves more than the act of committing physical violence against Blacks. White supremacy operates in business suits, through decisions made in the boardrooms of corporations; through the laws and policies enacted on the senate and congressional floors, and at the state and local level; in the structure and administration of the public school system and at colleges and universities; in courtrooms in the halls of *justice*; and through law enforcement, to name a few. White supremacy affects every aspect of life in America, and is most detrimental to Black life. According to Dr. Kevin W. Cosby, pastor of St. Stephen Baptist Church and president of Simmons College of Kentucky, a historically Black college and university, "White supremacy is the mythology that everything great, and of importance, and of significance in America was created by Whites, and if this greatness and importance is going to be sustained, Whites must continue to be in control."

Dr. Cosby went on to say, "The race problem cannot be eradicated until the attitude that Whites must be in control is eliminated." In other words, the Apostle Paul says, we must be transformed by the renewing of our minds. Consequently, Whites and all ethnic groups, including Blacks, are encouraged to take a moment after each devotional reading, for introspection in regard to your views and relationship with Black people as it pertains to the question asked; especially reflect on your relationship with Blacks who are the American Descendants of Slavery (ADOS), as opposed to Black immigrants who voluntarily came to America from another country, as ADOS are the bottom caste in America and are despised. Historically, Blacks are in the company of Jesus of whom Scripture says in this Messianic prophecy, "He was despised and rejected by mankind, a man of suffering, and familiar with pain. Like one from whom people hid their faces he was despised, and we held him in low esteem" (Isa. 53:3 NIV).

I encourage you to share this devotional book within your circles of influence—with spiritual partners, members across faith traditions, organization members, friends, and family members. During these forty days, you may want to join with others on a video conference and read the daily reflections together, or gather weekly to discuss how you've been affected by this Lenten experience. Resources to facilitate group study and preaching on this material are available for free download at www.wjkbooks.com /LentOfLiberation. You may want to organize a worship service to communally lament America's 400-plus years of injustice and pray for the liberation of American Descendants of Slavery. In 2019, on the occasion of the 400th anniversary of African slaves' arrival in the British colonies, St. Stephen Baptist Church in Louisville, Kentucky, and Simmons College of Kentucky (America's 107th and Kentucky's oldest historically Black college and university) held a 400th year commemoration ceremony engaging

Blacks and Whites of all ages and faith traditions in a litany of repentance, forgiveness, and reconciliation to the truth. Acknowledgement of the truth is the necessary first step to reconciliation. Complete reconciliation between Blacks and Whites in America comes when Whites become advocates in the fight against systemic racial injustices and in the call for reparations, and when justice is finally given to the American Descendants of Slavery. The twenty-page program for this ceremony, with litanies, readings, Scripture passages, and songs, is available for purchase online and can be adapted for your context.[5] Be encouraged to join with those of other races and ethnicities, and let the purpose in our hearts and the work of our hands be united for racial justice.

Day 1

[T]hese mothers, with their handsome daughters, were valued on the ledger of their owners at enormously high prices; that lustful traders and sensualists had already gloated over the thought of buying them in a few short years. Probably not one of those beautiful girls would have brought less than fifteen hundred or two thousand dollars at the age of fifteen. It was therefore a great satisfaction to think, that their mothers, who knew full well to what a fate such slave girls were destined, had labored so heroically to snatch them out of this danger ere the critical hour arrived.

> —The True Story of Rebecca Jones and
> Her Three Daughters, Sarah Frances,
> Mary, and Rebecca, and Caroline Taylor,
> and her two daughters, Nancy, and Mary

So I bought her for fifteen shekels of silver and a homer of barley and a measure of wine. And I said to her, "You must remain as mine for many days; you shall not play the whore, you shall not have intercourse with a man, nor I with you."

> —*Hosea 3:2–3*

In this biblical passage, Hosea's wife is on the auction block at a diminished value. It was the same with these five captive girls. The price paid for them might be high, but their value as human beings was diminished by their treatment as mere objects to be sold, placed on an auction block for the purpose of creating profit. Some were enslaved as profit generators; some (women) were enslaved as pleasure generators. These girls in the opening narrative were pleasure generators, the same as Gomer. The price paid for Gomer is miniscule because she had become devalued.

The only man who would purchase Gomer was Hosea, although she had no monetary value. The fact that Hosea wanted her is what gave her actual value in society. The fact that he committed himself to her with *hesed*, an unending, covenantal form of love, gave her value. Hosea's love was not exploitive, because the prophet declares his loyalty to Gomer: "You are to live with me many days; you must not be a prostitute or be intimate with any man, and I will behave the same way toward you" (v. 3 NIV).

There's a possibility that in her patriarchal society, Gomer could not survive without dependence on a man. Perhaps she had no option but to sell herself into Slavery. When American chattel Slavery ended, because reparations were not given to the enslaved, many had to sell themselves back into enslavement as sharecroppers simply to survive.

Some are quick to condemn Black people who have put themselves in situations like Gomer's, but they fail to address the systems and structures that force people into such desperate situations. They are in a survival mode. Gomer was in survival mode in a survivalist culture. Some Whites believe that Blacks sell drugs or engage in prostitution or other illegal behavior because of a degenerate culture. To be Black swimming against the tide of systemic racism often means to have no options. We thereby create the Gomers. It is survival.

We will never understand Black America's present circumstances without understanding past and present injustices and exclusion. This is what we will seek to do in these
forty reflections.

> *What Black organizations or Black activists can you con-
> nect with to better understand the unjust laws and poli-
> cies that contribute to high crime in Black communities?*

> *In what ways can you use your platform or influence to
> advocate for just policies for Black people?*

FACTS ABOUT BLACK OPPRESSION
First Arrivals

When John Rolfe wrote in his diary that "twenty
negars" arrived in Virginia in 1619, it was evidence
of the earliest presence of Africans in the English
colony. This was one year before the pilgrims landed
at Plymouth Rock in the Mayflower, but nearly one
hundred years after blacks had been in Spanish and
Portuguese colonies. . . . So vast an operation was
the European Slave Trade that it ravaged towns and
villages along the West African coast, and the inte-
rior, for three centuries of dogged destruction of the
African homeland to build a white homeland in the
ancestral territory of another people.

Molefi Kete Asante, *The African American People: A Global History* (New York:
Routledge, 2012), 41–42.

Day 2

Years before her escape, her mistress died in England; and as Rebecca had always understood, long before this event, that all the slaves were to be freed at the death of her mistress, she was not prepared to believe any other report. It turned out, however, as in thousands of other instances, that no will could be found, and, of course, the administrators retained the slave property, regardless of any verbal expressions respecting freeing, etc.

—The True Story of Rebecca Jones and
Her Three Daughters, Sarah Frances,
Mary, and Rebecca, and Caroline Taylor,
and her two daughters, Nancy, and Mary

Then the Lord said to Moses, "Pharaoh's heart is hardened; he refuses to let the people go."

—Exodus 7:14

Dr. Martin Luther King Jr. states in his "Letter from Birmingham Jail," "We know through painful experience that freedom is never voluntarily given by the oppressor; it must be demanded by the oppressed."[1]

Pharaoh became intoxicated with the power and wealth derived from free, exploited labor. He was Israel's oppressor and refused to release them from bondage. Oppressed people cannot afford the luxury of waiting until the oppressor is converted.

In Rebecca Jones's situation, promises that were made were not kept. Oppressors, when given the choice, refused to release their enslaved from bondage. Further, there is no historical evidence that Whites have ever voluntarily treated Blacks humanely or justly without radical provocation from Blacks.

We would be prudent to listen to the wisdom of Frederick Douglass:

> Power concedes nothing without a demand. It never did and it never will. Find out just what any people will quietly submit to and you have found out the exact measure of injustice and wrong which will be imposed upon them, and these will continue till they are resisted with either words or blows, or with both. The limits of tyrants are prescribed by the endurance of those whom they oppress.[2]

Although the protests that erupted across this nation in late May and early June, 2020, were in response to the blatant disregard for Black life in the sadistic and calculated killing of George Floyd by a Minneapolis policeman, it can also be said that the protests are a result of centuries of brutalization and systemic oppression levied against Black people. In the words of Dr. Martin Luther King Jr., "A riot is the language of the unheard."[3]

Have you ever been guilty of thinking, "Why now?" as it pertains to the demand for justice for African Americans (specifically American Descendants of Slavery)?

Perhaps a better question that one might answer is, "Why not now?"

Day 3

Isaiah, who was a fellow-servant with Rebecca, and was included in the reward offered by Hall for Rebecca, etc., was a young man about twenty-three years of age, a mulatto, intelligent and of prepossessing manners. A purely ardent thirst for liberty prompted him to flee; although he declared that he had been treated very badly and had even suffered severely from being shamefully "beaten." He had, however, been permitted to hire his time by the year, for which one hundred and twenty dollars were regularly demanded by his owner. Young as he was, he was a married man, with a wife and two children, to whom he was devoted. He had besides two brothers and two sisters for whom he felt a warm degree of brotherly affection; yet when the hour arrived for him to accept a chance for freedom at the apparent sacrifice of these dearest ties of kindred, he was found heroic enough for this painful ordeal, and to give up all for freedom.

—The True Story of Isaiah Robinson

Then God said, "Let us make humankind in our image, according to our likeness; and let them have dominion over the fish of the sea, and over the birds of the air, and over the cattle, and over all the wild animals of the earth, and over every creeping thing that creeps upon the earth."

—Genesis 1:26

God made humankind in God's image, giving them domin-ion—which means rule, dominate, control. The Genesis writer details what humankind is to control. Adam is to be the steward over creation—fish, birds, livestock, all creatures. The list does not include other humans. God appointed human beings to steward God's created world, but God did not grant authority to rule other mortals.

In 1851, Samuel Cartwright, a New Orleans doctor, published "Diseases and Peculiarities of the Negro Race" in *DeBow's Review*, a magazine concerned primarily with agriculture and industry in the South that had a decidedly proslavery bent.[1] The diseases in his report afflicted only Black people. One such ailment was a nonsensical form of mental illness called *drapetomania* (from the Greek word *drapetes*, which means to run away, and *mania*, which is Greek for madness or frenzy). The condition, which has since been debunked as pseudoscience, claimed that cer-tain Black people had an illness that caused them to flee enslavement because they desired freedom. Cartwright theorized that enslavement was a natural state for Blacks and any Black person who wanted to be free suffered from a form of mental illness.

I'm sure Cartwright would have diagnosed Isaiah Rob-inson with a severe case of *drapetomania*. The impulse to be self-determining is so strong that Isaiah Robinson was willing to sacrifice all that was important to him; namely, his family. Robinson's life story highlights that innate to the human condition is a quest for self-determination—the right to define oneself and determine one's destiny, instead of having one's identity and destiny defined and determined by others. There has never been a time in American history where Blacks, in the aggregate, have been self-determined.

Let us never forget that people of African descent are not listed among the category groups over which human-kind is given dominion in Genesis 1:26. Blacks are made in the image of God. Blacks are made to rule and to be self-determined and not to be other-determined.

Reflect on your personal, social, business, and faith networks. How can the decision-making processes around you be transformed, as it pertains to the welfare or destiny of Blacks, to listen to Black ideas, and to actually include Blacks in the decision making for their own well-being as opposed to the paternalistic approach?

An Economy Built on Our Backs

Eighty percent of all the cotton grown in the United States was exported across the Atlantic, almost all of it to Britain. Cotton was the most important raw material of the industrial revolution that created our modern world economy. . . . Cotton also drove US expansion, enabling the young country to grow from a narrow coastal belt into a vast, powerful nation with the fastest-growing economy in the world. Between the 1790s and 1820, the United States acquired a near-monopoly on the world's most widely traded commodity, and after 1820, cotton accounted for a majority of all US exports.

Edward E. Baptist, *The Half Has Never Been Told: Slavery and the Making of American Capitalism* (New York: Basic Books, 2014), 113.

Growing international demand for cotton fueled the growth of slavery, and the legal and political arms of the state maintained and protected it. More cotton led to more profits, which led to more demand for slaves, which led to more legislation supporting slavery, and then even crueler methods of oppression to extract more work from slaves. . . . Slavery modernized credit markets, creating complex new forms of financial instruments and trade networks through which slaves could be mortgaged, exchanged, and used as leverage to purchase more slaves.

Mehrsa Baradaran, *The Color of Money: Black Banks and the Racial Wealth Gap* (Cambridge, MA: The Belknap Press of Harvard University Press, 2017), 10–11.

Day 4

Ben was also a slave in North Carolina—located at Eatontown, being the property of "Miss Ann Blunt, who was very hard." In slave property Miss Blunt was interested to the number of about "ninety head." She was much in the habit of hiring out servants, and in thus disposing of her slaves Ben thought she was a great deal more concerned in getting good prices for herself than good places for them. Indeed he declared that "she did not care how mean the place was, if she could only get her price." For three years Ben had Canada and the Underground Rail Road in view, having been "badly treated." At last the long-looked for time arrived, and he conferred neither with master nor mistress, but "picked himself up" and "took out." Age twenty-eight, medium size, quite dark, a good carpenter, and generally intelligent. Left two sisters, etc.

—The True Story of Ben Dickinson

Now a certain man was ill, Lazarus of Bethany, the village of Mary and her sister Martha.

—John 11:1

The story of Ben and his two sisters is reminiscent of Lazarus and his two sisters, Mary and Martha, in John 11. Just as Mary and Martha were unmarried sisters who survived during ancient patriarchal times, the two sisters Ben left behind were in a state of triple jeopardy—enslaved black women. Their race, their gender, and their lack of economic standing made them quite vulnerable.

The raising of Lazarus guaranteed that his two sisters would have male protection. Conversely, the raising of Ben out of Slavery only exacerbated the vulnerabilities of the two sisters he left behind. One can only wonder how they fared in his absence, and whether they ever were able to reconcile at the end of the Civil War. After Emancipation, thousands of classified ads for Black family members seeking to reunite with parents, siblings, children, spouses, and other relatives appeared in newspapers across the country. These families were ripped apart by Slavery—babies were snatched from mothers, wives were taken from husbands, and siblings were taken from each other—all without their consent. The evil of Slavery gave Black people no good options.

Today, many Black families are separated by the crisis of mass incarceration. According to Michelle Alexander, in her book *The New Jim Crow: Mass Incarceration in the Age of Colorblindness*:

> The United States imprisons a larger percentage of its black population than South Africa did at the height of apartheid. In Washington, D.C., our nation's capitol, it is estimated that three out of four young black men (and nearly all those in the poorest neighborhoods) can expect to serve time in prison. Similar rates of incarceration can be found in black communities across America.[1]

Either Black men in the U.S. are the most innate criminals in world history, or the American system of justice is one of the most inhumane anti-Black systems in history.

So whether it is slavery or mass incarceration, White supremacy has always found a way to separate Ben from his two sisters.

A consequence of mass incarceration is that Black families are broken — children, wives, and loved ones are broken emotionally and economically. In what ways can you advocate for criminal justice reform?

What role can you assume in providing support to the Black families of the incarcerated? How can you be a source of hope for their children?

Day 5

Jacob Hall, alias Henry Thomas, wife Henrietta, and child, were also among the December passengers. On the subject of freedom they were thoroughly converted. Although Jacob was only about twenty years of age, he had seen enough of Slavery under his master, "Major William Hutchins," whom he described as a "farmer, commissioner, drunkard, and hard master," to know that no hope could be expected from him, but if he remained, he would daily have to be under the "harrow." The desire to work for himself was so strong, that he could not reconcile his mind to the demands of Slavery. While meditating upon freedom, he concluded to make an effort with his wife and child to go to Canada. . . . Their little child they resolved to cling to through thick and thin; so, in order that they might not have so far to carry him, father and mother each bridled a horse and "took out" in the direction of the first Underground Rail Road station.

—The True Story of Jacob Hall
(Alias Henry Thomas), Wife,
Henrietta, and Child

And he brought forth the people that were therein, and put them under saws, and under harrows of iron, and under axes of iron, and made them pass through the brick-kiln: and thus did he unto all the cities of the children of Ammon. So David and all the people returned unto Jerusalem.

—2 Samuel 12:31 KJV

Many of the biblical heroes behaved in a less-than-heroic manner. It is important when interpreting the Bible to remember that not everything that is descriptive is *prescriptive*. For example, in the book of Leviticus, many of the dietary laws abstaining from pork and shellfish were part of the holiness codes designed to make Israel distinctive from Israel's Palestinian neighbors. Just because the writer in Leviticus describes dietary laws, the prohibition of clothing made of two different garments and the prohibiting of women from entering the tabernacle during their menstrual cycle does not mean that the Bible is prescribing these practices for us today. What ultimately determines what is descriptive and prescriptive is the ethics of Jesus.

Since Jesus is the standard, this story in 2 Samuel 12:31, of David enslaving the Ammonites and forcing them to become human draft animals pulling harrows, describes where David was ethically, but it does not prescribe what Christians should practice. Pulling the harrow is what motivated Jacob Hall to escape from Slavery. Had he remained, he would have been under the harrow daily — his life would be likened to that of a draft animal.

We do not know if Jacob and Henrietta's child was a male or female. We do know this — had the child been a male, he too would one day be pulling the harrow as a human ox. Jacob Hall's escape from such brutality not only removed him but also his descendants from the harrow.

When you see or hear of injustices, do you relate to the news only from a descriptive point of view?

How can you go beyond what is described about Black injustices to understanding the root causes, and then to work for justice as the Bible prescribes?

What steps will you take the next time you learn of an unjust situation in your local community?

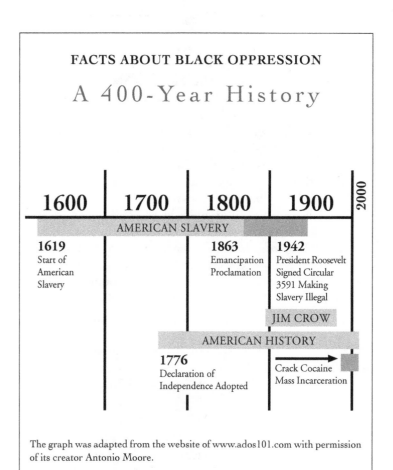

FACTS ABOUT BLACK OPPRESSION

A 400-Year History

1600	1700	1800	1900	2000

AMERICAN SLAVERY

1619
Start of American Slavery

1863
Emancipation Proclamation

1942
President Roosevelt Signed Circular 3591 Making Slavery Illegal

JIM CROW

AMERICAN HISTORY

1776
Declaration of Independence Adopted

Crack Cocaine
Mass Incarceration

The graph was adapted from the website of www.ados101.com with permission of its creator Antonio Moore.

Day 6

James Hamlet was the first slave case who was summarily arrested under the Fugitive Slave Law, and sent back to bondage from New York. William and Ellen Craft were hotly pursued to Boston by hunters from Georgia. Adam Gibson, a free colored man, residing in Philadelphia, was arrested, delivered into the hands of his alleged claimants, by commissioner Edward D. Ingraham, and hurried into Slavery. Euphemia Williams (the mother of six living children), her case excited much interest and sympathy. Shadrach was arrested and rescued in Boston. Hannah Dellum and her child were returned to Slavery from Philadelphia. Thomas Hall and his wife were pounced upon at midnight in Chester County, beaten and dragged off to Slavery, etc.

> —The True Story of James Hamlet,
> William and Ellen Craft, Adam Gibson,
> Euphemia Williams, Shadrach,
> Hannah Dellum and Her Child,
> Thomas Hall and His Wife

Where can I go from your spirit? Or where can I flee from your presence? If I ascend to heaven, you are there; if I make my bed in Sheol, you are there. If I take the wings of the

*morning and settle at the farthest limits of the sea, even there
your hand shall lead me, and your right hand shall hold me
fast. If I say, "Surely the darkness shall cover me, and the
light around me become night," even the darkness is not dark
to you; the night is as bright as the day, for darkness is as
light to you.*

—*Psalm 139:7–12*

There is a Negro spiritual that goes:

> Dere's no hidin' place down dere,
> Dere's no hidin' place down dere.
> Oh, I went to the rock to hide my face,
> The rock cried out, "No hidin' place";
> Dere's no hidin' place down dere.[1]

Undoubtedly, this is how all Blacks felt after the passing of the Fugitive Slave Law of 1850—both those free and enslaved, throughout the United States. This law was, without question, the worst piece of legislation ever enacted against Black America. It not only undermined the work of the Underground Railroad, but it also endangered free Blacks living in the North who could be kidnapped and sold into enslavement.

Psalm 139 speaks of the ubiquitous presence of God. With the passing of the Fugitive Slave Law, what seemed to be ubiquitous was not the presence of God, but rather, the presence of White supremacy and oppression.

How does one maintain hope and belief in an all-loving, all-powerful God in light of such atrocities? One of the often-overlooked realities among the enslaved is the presence of atheism. It is often assumed that the enslaved were theistic, but there was always a thread of atheism within the Black community during Slavery.

If the idea of God died in the consciousness of enslaved Blacks, it is because White supremacy killed the understanding of a God who is loving, powerful, and just.

In protest movements for racial justice, there is a slogan that says, "White silence = White consent." Have you been silent in the face of Black suffering, poverty, and despair?

What can you do to challenge this narrative, lift others, and bring hope?

FACTS ABOUT BLACK OPPRESSION

Chattel Slavery

Europe also practiced indenture and serfdom. Neither of these forms of service, one with a time period attached to it, and the other with land attached to it, could be compared to the chattel slavery of Africans. Serfdom is not the same as slavery. Sometimes this is confused in the mind of the contemporary person. The current usage of the term chattel slavery is not synonymous with serfdom. Enslaved Africans were people who had neither rights nor freedom of movement, and were not paid for their labor because they were seen as "things." Aside from providing food and shelter, the enslaver had no responsibility to the enslaved, but would allow the enslaved no space to have responsibility for him or herself.

Molefi Kete Asante, *The African American People: A Global History* (New York: Routledge, 2012), 60.

Day 7

Lewis was described as a light yellow man, medium size, good-looking, and intelligent. In referring to bondage, he spoke with a great earnestness, and in language very easily understood; especially when speaking of Samuel Myers, from whom he escaped, he did not hesitate to give him the character of being a very hard man, who was never satisfied, no matter how hard the slaves might try to please him. Myers was engaged in the commission and forwarding business, and was a man of some standing in Richmond. From him Lewis had received very severe floggings, the remembrance of which he would not only carry with him to Canada, but to the grave.

—The True Story of Lewis Cobb

Five times I have received from the Jews the forty lashes minus one.

—2 Corinthians 11:24

Paul records that he was beaten five times and that he received thirty-nine lashes each time, which is a total of 195 times. Paul is recounting this to the Corinthian church to establish his credibility as an apostle and servant leader of the Lord Jesus Christ.

One of the most striking images from Slavery is that of a formerly enslaved man revealing his severely lacerated back that was the result of a flogging he had received.[1] As much as we may attempt to sanitize Slavery, it was a heinous, brutal institution. Plantations were arsenals of inhumane torture. According to William A. Darity Jr. and A. Kirsten Muellen, "The slaves are often tortured by iron collars, with long prongs or 'horns' and sometimes bells attached to them—they are made to wear chains, handcuffs, fetters, iron clogs, bars, rings, and bands of iron upon their limbs, iron masks upon their faces, iron gags in their mouths, etc."[2]

No wonder Lewis Cobb said he would carry the flogging he received from Samuel Myers to his grave. We will never know the extent of the physical and psychological damage Cobb endured for the rest of his life. The fact that Paul mentioned his wounds to the Corinthian believers means that the psychological scars he endured survived long past the physical pain.

Lewis Cobb's back expressed the physical damage he endured many years after the incident. We can never truly know the extent of the psychological trauma inflicted by the severe flogging that he took to his grave.

How can you quiet your voice in order to listen to the voice of African Americans and their daily realities and sufferings endured under oppression?

In what ways can you demonstrate solidarity and uplift?

Day 8

Major Latham was forty-four years of age, mulatto, very resolute, with good natural abilities, and a decided hater of slavery. John Latham was the man whom he addressed as "master," which was a very bitter pill for him to swallow. He had been married twice, and at the time of his escape he was the husband of two wives. The first one, with their three children, in consequence of changes incident to slave life, was sold a long distance from her old home and husband, thereby ending the privilege of living together; he could think of them but that was all; he was compelled to give them up altogether. After a time he took to himself another wife, with whom he lived several years. Three more children owned him as father—the result of this marriage. During his entire manhood Major had been brutally treated by his master, which caused him a great deal of anguish and trouble of mind. Only a few weeks before he escaped, his master, in one of his fits of passion, flogged him most cruelly. From that time the resolution was permanently grounded in his mind to find the way to freedom.

—The True Story of Major Latham

"Now there were seven brothers among us; the first married, and died childless, leaving the widow to his brother. The second did the same, so also the third, down to the seventh. Last of all, the woman herself died."

—Matthew 22:25–27

Jesus was once asked about a woman who had seven husbands, all of them brothers—and then she also died. Levirate law specified that when a man died, his brother was supposed to marry the widow. The seven husbands died, which means this woman was passed to seven different men. The Sadducees, who did not believe in the resurrection, asked Jesus which of the seven brothers the woman would be married to in heaven.

In a sense, Major Latham has a similar dilemma as the seven brothers in the story that the Sadducees told Jesus. Who is he married to? Who will be his wife after the Civil War is over?

Many White evangelicals—who defended the enslavement of Black people—promote the idea of one man and one wife for one lifetime. The hypocrisy of White pro-slavery Christianity is that it put Black people in positions where they could never live according to the ethics preached in the Christian faith—and when Christian ethics would seem to support liberation, White Christians rejected those interpretations. A prime example of this would be spiritualizing biblical texts on justice, such as Jesus' sermon in Luke 4:18, "The Spirit of the Lord is upon me, because he has anointed me to bring good news to the poor." The word poor in this text (*ptochos*) literally means those who are experiencing economic destitution—beggars or paupers. Interpreting this word to mean spiritual poverty, White evangelicals today avoid addressing the problem of racial wealth inequality, focusing instead on personal pietism independent of concrete demands for justice.

There are no value-neutral hermeneutics. Every interpreter of Scripture often reads into Scripture one's own economic and social location. We are often too reluctant to interpret Scripture that conflicts with our privileges. That is why the hermeneutics of the oppressed can never be the hermeneutics of the oppressor. That is why if the oppressed are to be free, they can never embrace the hermeneutics of their oppressor. Women cannot allow patriarchy to interpret Scripture for them. LGBTQ persons cannot allow straight evangelical White males to interpret Scripture for them. American Descendants of Slavery must reject White hermeneutics if ADOS are to be liberated from oppression.

Have you rejected Christianity or the Bible based on the stated interpretations made by White evangelicals or leaders who have close associations with them?

Day 9

Belinda was a large woman, thirty years of age, wholly black, and fled from Mr. Hyson, in company with William, and those above referred to, with the idea of reaching Canada, whither her father had fled eight years before. She was evidently pleased with the idea of getting away from her ill-natured mistress, from poor fare and hard work without pay. She had experienced much hardship, and had become weary of her trial in bondage. She had been married, but her husband had died, leaving her two little girls to care for, both of whom she succeeded in bringing away with her. In reference to the church relations of her master and mistress, she represented the former as a backslider, and added that money was his church; of the latter she said, "she would go and take the sacrament, come back and the old boy would be in her as big as a horse." Belinda could see but little difference between her master and mistress.

— The True Story of Belinda Bivans

Ahab told Jezebel all that Elijah had done, and how he had killed all the prophets with the sword. Then Jezebel sent a messenger to Elijah, saying, "So may the gods do to me, and more also, if I do not make your life like the life of one of them by this time tomorrow."

— 1 Kings 19:1–2

Jezebel wanted to kill Elijah because he had wiped out her 450 prophets of Baal. The word Baal literally meant master. Jezebel had introduced Baalism—the belief that some were destined to be masters possessing the ultimate power of life and death—into Israel. Those not becoming masters were intended to be servants who were subject to the wishes of the Baal, the master. Jezebel's sin is often thought to be seduction (because in White evangelicalism the ultimate sin is always something sexual in nature), but the real crime of Jezebel was the idolatrous system of Baalism that made some masters and others slaves.

We often think that Slavery was primarily a White man's institution, but historian Stephanie E. Jones-Rogers argues quite persuasively in *They Were Her Property: White Women as Slave Owners in the American South*, that "slave owning [white] women not only witnessed the most brutal features of slavery, they took part in them, profited from them and defended them. . . . White women might punish enslaved people. They might even be brutal and sadistic."[1] Jones-Rogers calls them "mistresses of the market."

Ona Judge was one of George Washington's slaves. She escaped to the North and evaded capture, though he and Martha pursued her until George's death.[2] While we know that George Washington owned 300 slaves, the majority of those slaves—including Ona—came through his wife, Martha. While we consider Martha to be the first lady of the nation, through the lens of ADOS, she was the first Jezebel of the nation.

In what way has propaganda been used historically and currently in the media and education system to portray White innocence and Black guilt?

How can you challenge these distorted portrayals on a consistent basis?

FACTS ABOUT BLACK OPPRESSION

European Complicity

Prior to 1807 the British Parliament passed numerous laws and regulations to encourage and support the trade in human beings. . . . One cannot forget, even if one wanted to, that in Liverpool the economy thrived on the building of slave ships and the transport of Africans from the continent to the Americas. Nothing is more authentic at this moment in history than the recognition that a great wrong was done to African people and that cities such as Bristol, Nantes, Bordeaux, Lisbon, and Liverpool stood in the center of the chaos on one side of the ocean as Charleston, Savannah, Norfolk, Philadelphia, Baltimore, and New Orleans stood in the center in North America.

Molefi Kete Asante, *The African American People: A Global History* (New York: Routledge, 2012), 64.

The bonds created by southwestern states [the states of the U.S.]—each one a guarantee of an income stream from the labor of mortgaged hands—found buyers in all of the major financial centers in the Western world—London, New York, Philadelphia, Amsterdam, Hamburg, Bremen, and Paris. Investors around the world voted their confidence in slavery's expansion. And rising London prices for southwestern securities, statistics demonstrate, pushed up slave prices in New Orleans.

Edward E. Baptist, *The Half Has Never Been Told: Slavery and the Making of American Capitalism* (New York: Basic Books, 2014), 256.

Day 10

Silas was quite black, spare-built and about twenty-seven years of age. He was owned by Sheriff Robert Bell, a man about "sixty years of age, and had his name up to be the hardest man in the county. . . . The Sheriff's wife was about pretty much such a woman as he was a man—there was not a pin's point of difference between them." The fear of having to be sold caused this Silas to seek the Underground Rail Road. Leaving his mother, one brother and one cousin, and providing himself with a Bowie-knife and a few dollars in money, he resolved to reach Canada, "or die on the way." Of course, when slaves reached this desperate point, the way to Canada was generally found.

—The True Story of Silas Long

One day, as we were going to the place of prayer, we met a slave-girl who had a spirit of divination and brought her owners a great deal of money by fortune-telling. While she followed Paul and us, she would cry out, "These men are slaves of the Most High God, who proclaim to you a way of salvation." She kept doing this for many days. But Paul, very much annoyed, turned and said to the spirit, "I order you in the name of Jesus Christ to come out of her." And it came out that very hour. But when her owners saw that their hope of making money was gone, they seized Paul and Silas and dragged them into the marketplace before the authorities.

—Acts 16:16–19

How appropriate that this enslaved man's name was Silas, for he was in many ways like the colleague and understudy of the Apostle Paul. The familiar biblical story of Paul and Silas incarcerated in a Philippian dungeon at midnight tells how the men—with bloodied backs, and manacled ankles and wrists—sang praises to God. What is often overlooked in their story are the factors that put Paul and Silas in this predicament. We are told in Acts 16:16 that they had liberated a slave girl who brought much profit to her master. Slavery brought much profit to America. The value of the enslaved community was worth more than all the combined worth of the railroads, banks, and businesses in America—3.2 million slaves were worth $1.3 billion in market value, almost equal to the entire gross national product.[1]

The enslaved Silas in our story had many similarities to the Silas in Acts 16. Both had an utter disdain for Slavery and both were willing to pay whatever price necessary for it to be destroyed.

In what ways does the legacy of the past foster continued White advantage and Black disadvantage?

Can there be justice without reparations?

FACTS ABOUT BLACK OPPRESSION

J.U.S.T.I.C.E. =
Reparations, A Debt Owed

This acrostic, created by Dr. Kevin Cosby, captures with profound simplicity why reparations is a debt owed to the American Descendants of Slavery. The targeted mistreatment of the enslaved in America has continued well into the twenty-first century for their descendants—the American Descendants of Slavery. As mentioned earlier, Dr. Martin Luther King Jr. espoused that since ADOS were targeted with special mistreatment, ADOS should be targeted for special treatment. Reparations is not a handout. It is a debt owed.

J – Jim Crow
U – Urban Renewal
S – Slavery
T – Terrorism (Lynchings; George Floyd was a
    public lynching in 2020)
I – Incarceration (Mass)
C – Cops, Courts (Kill Blacks with impunity)
E – Exclusions (Restrictions to home ownership,
    barriers to land purchase, discriminatory
    lending practices, etc.)

—Rev. Dr. Kevin W. Cosby, St. Stephen Baptist Church, Louisville, KY

Day 11

Jane did not know how old she was. She was probably sixty or seventy. She fled to keep from being sold. She had been "whipt right smart," poorly fed and poorly clothed, by a certain Roger McZant, of the New Market District, Eastern Shore of Maryland. His wife was a "bad woman too." Just before escaping, Jane got a whisper that her "master" was about to sell her; on asking him if the rumor was true, he was silent. He has been asking "one hundred dollars" for her. Remembering that four of her children had been snatched away from her and sold South, and she herself was threatened with the same fate, she was willing to suffer hunger, sleep in the woods for nights and days, wandering towards Canada, rather than trust herself any longer under the protection of her "kind" owner. . . . Jane, doubtless, represented thousands of old slave mothers, who, after having been worn out under the yoke, were frequently either offered for sale for a trifle, turned off to die, or compelled to eke out their existence on the most stinted allowance.

—The True Story of Jane Davis

"So I say to you: Ask and it will be given to you; seek and you will find; knock and the door will be opened to you."

—Luke 11:9 NIV

Frederick Douglass once said that he prayed and asked God to deliver him from slavery. He said God never answered that prayer, but one day Douglass decided to pray with his feet. So he ran away and God answered his prayer. This is what Jane did also. Her description of being whipped, her children being sold, and her imminent sale no doubt caused her to pray. It was not until she prayed with her feet that God answered her prayer.

Jesus said "ask," which means to petition. But he also said seek, which is petition plus effort, or in the case of Jane and Frederick Douglass, petitioning using your feet. Knock means petition, plus effort, plus determination.

In early 2020, Breonna Taylor, a Black female EMT, was shot eight times and killed by police officers of the Louisville Metro Police Department, who had barged into her apartment unannounced through a no-knock warrant. Although this horrible incident occurred a couple of months prior to the George Floyd killing, it only came to light because of George Floyd's killing. The police department (which had mishandled the case in many ways in addition to the no-knock warrant) and the media kept it so quiet that a majority of Louisville residents did not know about Breonna Taylor. Once her unjustified murder went public, it could be said that hundreds of Louisvillians prayed with their feet, as they took to the streets in protest for Breonna and for George. After many days of relentless protests, and because of national attention, Breonna's Law was passed in Louisville, Kentucky, whereby no-knock warrants were banned.

Sometimes we believe God has not answered our prayers because we stop short of seeking and knocking for an answer.

Besides praying about Black oppression, what tangible things can you do to be an answer to your prayers?

When will you begin?

Day 12

Edward was about forty-four years of age, of unmixed blood, and in point of natural ability he would rank among the most intelligent of the oppressed class. Without owing thanks to any body he could read and write pretty well, having learned by his own exertions. Tabby and Eliza Fortlock, sisters, and single women, had been deriving years of leisure, comfort, and money from the sweat of Edward's brow. The maiden ladies owned about eighteen head of this kind of property, far more than they understood how to treat justly or civilly. They bore the name of being very hard to satisfy. They were proverbially "stingy." They were members of the Christ Episcopal Church.

— The True Story of Edward Haines

For the bed is too short to stretch oneself on it, and the covering too narrow to wrap oneself in it.

— *Isaiah 28:20*

When Isaiah says the cover is too narrow and the bed is too short, he is saying that the situation in which many people find themselves is too small for them. They can never be comfortable in a bed that is too short or warmed by a blanket that could never provide them with adequate covering.

For a person of intellectual capacity and aspirations to be treated as a household commodity or draft animal is like lying in a bed that is too short and wrapped with covers that are too small. Perhaps the greatest crime Slavery committed against Black people was that it dwarfed and undermined their ability to grow intellectually and inspirationally into the full measure of a person.

The United Negro College Fund's motto wisely cautions, "A mind is a terrible thing to waste." It was reported that Edward had natural abilities and was most intelligent. Not only was Edward robbed of his right to self-actualize, society was robbed of the benefits his developed gifts might have brought to society.

Historically Black colleges and universities (HBCU) are 4 percent of the colleges in the United States, but they graduate in the baccalaureate degree about 28 percent of all Black students; 50 percent of all Black public school teachers are trained at HBCUs; 75 percent of all Black doctors, physicians, and engineers are trained at HBCUs.[1] HBCUs are a valuable jewel to our nation; however, the great challenge for HBCUs is that they reflect the economic situation of Black America. Black America does not have much wealth. For every dollar that White families have, Black families possess 10 percent."[2] Expanding on the UNCF motto, "A mind is a terrible thing to waste, but it's also a wonderful thing to invest in."

While the majority of PWIs (predominantly White institutions) thrive and are heavily endowed, the majority of HBCUs operate on a shoestring budget and barely survive. Additionally, private HBCUs receive even less support. In what ways can people of good will help to keep our nation's HBCUs strong?

Day 13

Harriet had treasured up a heavy account against a white man known by the name of William A. Linton, whom she described as a large, red-faced man, who had in former years largely invested in slave property, but latterly he had been in the habit of selling off, until only seven remained, and among them she and her child were numbered; therefore, she regarded him as one who had robbed her of her rights, and daily threatened her with sale. Harriet was a very likely-looking woman, twenty-nine years of age, medium size, and of a brown color, and far from being a stupid person. Her daughter also was a smart, and interesting little girl of eight years of age, and seemed much pleased to be getting out of the reach of slave-holders. The mother and daughter, however, had not won their freedom thus far, without great suffering, from the long and fatiguing distance which they were obliged to walk. Sometimes the hardness of the road made them feel as though they would be compelled to give up the journey, whether or not; but they added to their faith, patience, and thus finally succeeded.

—The True Story of Harriet Stewart and Her Daughter, Mary Eliza

My tears have been my food day and night, while people say
to me continually, "Where is your God?"

—Psalm 42:3

Many times, nonbelievers have the best arguments for the
nonexistence of God. In Psalm 42 a devout Jew is experiencing severe hardship. He is suffering and his tears have
become his food. While this is happening, some of his crit-
ics are gleefully taunting, "Where is your God?"

While the Bible clearly states that God is a very present help in times of trouble, for many enslaved Americans,
God seemed like a very absent help in the time of trouble.

Harriet likely felt no different than the writer of Psalm
42. Describing the hardships that she and her eight-year-
old daughter endured through the atrocities of enslavement, she no doubt wondered, "Where now is God?"

How do the enslaved connect to God in the midst of the
indescribable evil of Slavery?

God is present as we read Harriet's story in her passion
to be free as well as in her determination not to give up
the journey to freedom. She recalled, "The hardness of the
road made them feel as though they would be compelled to
give up the journey."

The strength not to give up—to keep on keeping on—is
the presence of God.

How might you connect the presence of God in the life of
African Americans who have, historically and regularly,
experienced systemic racism, profiling, police brutal-
ity, redlining, subprime lending, mass incarceration,
discriminatory practices, and unjust court sentences, to
name a few?

What might God be asking you to do in response?

Day 14

Bill providentially escaped from a well-known cripple, whom he undertook to describe as a "very sneaking-looking man, medium size, smooth face; a wealthy farmer, who owned eighteen or twenty head of slaves, and was Judge of the Orphans' Court." "He sells slaves occasionally." "My mistress was a very large, rough, Irish-looking woman, with a very bad disposition; it appeared like as if she hated to see a 'nigger,' and she was always wanting her husband to have some one whipped, and she was a member of the Methodist Church. My master was a trustee in the Episcopal Church."

—The True Story of Bill Cole

Remember that you were a slave in the land of Egypt, and the LORD your God redeemed you.

—*Deuteronomy 15:15*

Abraham Lincoln once said, "Those who think Slavery is not that bad ought to try it." His assumption was that personal experience would give us empathy, but that is not always the case. Bill Cole was the slave of a well-known crippled man. One might think that his own physical challenges would have given him empathy toward the enslaved. Instead, it hardened his heart. That is why God said to Israel, "Never forget that you were once a slave."

Firsthand knowledge of what oppression feels like should motivate us never to oppress others.

There once was a little boy whose father took him to the pet shop to buy a puppy. The little boy intentionally chose a puppy with a bum leg. The pet store owner tried to talk him out of it because the puppy would never be able to run with the boy. The little boy was resolute, "I want him!" He then rolled up his pant leg, revealing the brace on his leg. "I've got a bum leg too," he told the proprietor, "so I want the dog with the bum leg because he probably needs someone who understands."

Perhaps the greatest sign of spiritual maturity is the ability and desire to enter into someone else's world, live their real-life experience, and view reality through their lens. This is something that must be done intentionally. It often happens because we, ourselves, have experienced hurt, pain, and disappointment. For example, the reason the good Samaritan helped the victimized man on the Jericho road was because as a Samaritan in a Jewish world, he, too, had been victimized. He knew what it meant to be beat up, passed over, and left to die. While it is totally impossible for Whites to know the pressure of being Black in a world in which Whites define normality—and based on that definition, Blacks are abnormal in all things and in all ways—it is critical that Whites see Black suffering and pain as reality before Whites can enter into their pain. Whites must first be willing to acknowledge that the suffering exists and that they are responsible for its existence. Knowing the truth about White supremacy may hurt, but it's a necessary step in healing our racial divide.

How can you be intentional about entering into Black space to gain a greater understanding and empathize with racism or other "isms" experienced?

The way one enters Black space is important — enter, not to dictate, but enter with humility to learn. Listen.

FACTS ABOUT BLACK OPPRESSION

Negro Soldiers

In March of 1865, nearly two thirds of the Union troops in the Mississippi Valley were Negroes. Altogether about 180,000 Negroes served in the Union Army, where they comprised about 9 or 10 percent of the total enlistment. Nearly 50,000 were in the navy, amounting to about one quarter of the total naval forces. Negro servicemen faced hardships unknown to the white soldiers and sailors. One very serious problem was the Southern policy of either killing black soldiers and their white officers, even those who surrendered, or forcing the captured blacks into slavery. The most notorious instance followed the battle of Fort Pillow, on the Mississippi above Memphis, in April 1864. A rebel force captured the fort, and of the 262 Negroes stationed there, scores were massacred after surrendering.

August Meier and Elliott Rudwick, *From Plantation to Ghetto*, 3rd ed. (New York: Hill and Wang, 1976), 161.

Day 15

Elizabeth fled in company with her brother the winter previous to her arrival at the Philadelphia station. Although she reached free land the severe struggle cost her the loss of all her toes. Four days and nights out in the bitter cold weather without the chance of a fire left them a prey to the frost, which made sad havoc with their feet especially — particularly Elizabeth's. She was obliged to stop on the way, and for seven months she was unable to walk. Elizabeth was about twenty years of age, chestnut color, and of considerable natural intellect. Although she suffered so severely as the result of her resolution to throw off the yoke, she had no regrets at leaving the prison-house; she seemed to appreciate freedom all the more in consequence of what it cost her to obtain the prize.

— The True Story of Elizabeth Williams

Adoni-bezek fled; but they pursued him, and caught him, and cut off his thumbs and big toes.

— Judges 1:6

Warfare in Old Testament times could be quite cruel and inhumane. A good example of this is what was done to King Bezek in Judges 1:6. After he was defeated, Judah's army cut off both his thumbs and big toes. Without those two important toes, he could not stand or run. Without thumbs, he could not yield a sword, which meant they had disabled him for future battles.

When Elizabeth fled in the winter to escape the brutality of Slavery, something similar happened to her. The bitter cold weather caused frostbite and she lost all her toes. In the Bible, King Bezek had no choice. Elizabeth did. She was so hungry for freedom that—forced to choose between freedom and not having toes—she willingly sacrificed her toes for her freedom.

Elizabeth's willingness to be physically challenged without toes, believing she got a bargain in the deal, highlights the unimaginable horror and utter brutality of Slavery. The Negro spiritual *Nobody Knows the Trouble I've Seen* was the slave's way of poetically saying that it is truly inconceivable the pain Slavery inflicted both physically and psychologically on its victims. It is the greatest crime against humanity in recorded history. In a sense, Black people are still sacrificing their thumbs and toes in order to be free.

The recent rebellions that have erupted in our cities in which Blacks have endured pepper spray, rubber bullets, tasers, and incarceration is a collective determination of the Black community's strong desire to dismantle White supremacy even if it costs toes, hands, and even life.

What would you be willing to sacrifice to advocate for justice on behalf of African Americans?

In remembering the popular slogan, "White silence = White consent," are you willing to risk ridicule and scorn for speaking out and standing up along with African Americans?

What would make this sacrifice too high a price for you to pay?

Day 16

Edward, a youthful passenger about twenty-one years of age, slow of speech, with a stammering utterance, and apparently crushed in spirits, claimed succor and aid of the Committee. At first, the Committee felt a little puzzled to understand, how one, apparently so deficient, could succeed in surmounting the usual difficulties consequent upon traveling, via the Underground Rail Road; but in conversing with him, they found him possessed of more intelligence than they had supposed; indeed, they perceived that he could read and write a little, and that what he lacked in aptness of speech, he supplied as a thinker, and although he was slow he was sure. He was owned by a man named John Lewis, who . . . sold him, with two of his brothers, only the Saturday before his escape, to a Georgia trader, named Durant, who was to start south with them on the subsequent Monday. Moved almost to desperation at their master's course in thus selling them, the three brothers, after reflection, determined to save themselves if possible, and without any definite knowledge of the journey, they turned their eyes towards the North Star, and under the cover of night they started for Pennsylvania, not knowing whether they would ever see the goodly land of freedom.

—The True Story of Edward Carroll

But Moses said to the Lord, "O my Lord, I have never been eloquent, neither in the past nor even now that you have spoken to your servant; but I am slow of speech and slow of tongue."

—Exodus 4:10

Edward Carroll shocked his sponsors on the Underground Railroad. Besides being youthful, he possessed "stammering utterances." His inability to communicate left him with a great sense of inadequacy. He was "crushed in spirits." One cannot help but wonder if he ever heard the story about another man who hated Slavery as much as he did, and who also had a speech impediment.

When God called Moses to liberate the children of Israel from Slavery, one of the excuses he made for not obeying God was his lack of eloquence. God promised to be with him and to empower him to speak. What God was really saying to Moses was that he would learn how to speak by speaking.

Sometimes we want to wait until all conditions are right before we act. Edward Carroll acted toward his freedom while everything was not right. Because of his faith, God activated other gifts that never would have surfaced had he remained in Slavery. The sketch of his life says, "what he lacked in aptness of speech, he supplied as a thinker, and although he was slow he was sure."

According to Dr. Kevin W. Cosby, many Black youth are mislabeled, misdiagnosed, socially maladaptive, and treated as unassimiable and incorigible. The tragedy is that we do not simply believe this about them, but we have made them to believe this about themselves. How can you encourage and nourish the untapped potential of African American youth, many of whom don't believe that college is attainable for them?

Day 17

He had reached the age of thirty, and despite the opposition he had had to encounter, unaided he had learned to read, which with his good share of native intelligence, he found of service. Whilst Robert did not publish his mistress, he gave a plain statement of where he was from, and why he was found in the city of Brotherly Love in the dead of Winter in a state of destitution. He charged the blame upon a woman, whose name was Richardson, who, he said, was quite a "fighter, and was never satisfied, except when quarreling and fighting with some of the slaves." He also spoke of a certain T.J. Richardson, a farmer and a "very driving man" who was in the habit of oppressing poor men and women by compelling them to work in his tobacco, corn, and wheat fields without requiting them for their labor. Robert felt if he could get justice out of said Richardson he would be the gainer to the amount of more than a thousand dollars in money besides heavy damages for having cheated him out of his education. In this connection, he recalled the fact of Richardson's being a member of the church, and in a sarcastic manner added that his "religious pretensions might pass among slaveholders, but that it would do him no good when meeting the Judge above."

— The True Story of Robert Carr

Say therefore to the Israelites, "I am the LORD, and I will free you from the burdens of the Egyptians and deliver you from slavery to them. I will redeem you with an outstretched arm and with mighty acts of judgment. I will take you as my people, and I will be your God. You shall know that I am the LORD your God, who has freed you from the burdens of the Egyptians. I will bring you into the land that I swore to give to Abraham, Isaac, and Jacob; I will give it to you for a possession. I am the LORD."

—Exodus 6:6–8

Robert Carr believed in a God of justice. He recognized that those who have been empowered to oppress on earth will not be empowered to do the same in the afterlife. Carr also did not confuse religious practice with true discipleship and was undeterred by false piety.

Three types of justice can be seen here in Exodus 6:6–8. There is retributive justice—God punishes Egypt. Then there is restorative justice, which means God's promises to restore Israel as a nation. Finally, there is redistributive justice: God is taking them to the land and will redistribute the land.

African Americans have yet to experience each of these forms of justice. While no longer in legal bondage, far too many Blacks are constrained by economic, societal, and educational inequities. Many Blacks are in prison bondage or, as Douglas Blackmon refers to it, "Black reenslavement," which continues on in the twenty-first century. Although the Thirteenth Amendment officially abolished Slavery, Congress provided itself with an important loophole—no one can be held bound in servitude except for a crime. This tragic loophole became the basis for a new form of Slavery or, as it is often called, Slavery by another name: mass incarceration. Blacks are profiled and once charged with a crime find themselves in the prison industrial complex pipeline, their Black bodies kept in bondage and leased out to private businesses without pay for their work.[1] Nevertheless, many faithful believers, like Carr, trust that the injustices that prevail today will be nonexistent tomorrow.

> *How can you be an ambassador for justice — through either restorative justice or redistributive justice — on behalf of American Descendants of Slavery?*

> *How can you become a vocal advocate against mass incarceration that disproportionately targets Black males?*

Day 18

Plymouth was forty-two years of age, of a light chestnut color, with keen eyes, and a good countenance, and withal possessed of shrewdness enough to lead double the number that accompanied him. . . . The name of the man who had made merchandise of Plymouth was Nat Horsey, of Horsey's Cross Roads. The most striking characteristic in Horsey's character, according to Plymouth's idea was, that he was that very "hard to please, did not know when a slave did enough, had no idea that they could get tired or they needed any privileges." . . . When Plymouth parted with his wife with a "full heart," he bade her good-night, without intimating to her that he never expected to see her again in this world; she evidently supposed that he was going home to his master's place as usual, but instead he was leaving his companion and three children to wear the yoke as hitherto. He sympathized with them deeply, but felt that he could render them no real good remaining; he could neither live with his wife nor could he have any command over one of his children. Slavery demanded all, but allowed nothing.

— The True Story of Plymouth Cannon

Now after they had left, an angel of the Lord appeared to Joseph in a dream and said, "Get up, take the child and his

mother, and flee to Egypt, and remain there until I tell you;
for Herod is about to search for the child, to destroy him."
Then Joseph got up, took the child and his mother by night,
and went to Egypt, and remained there until the death of
Herod. This was to fulfill what had been spoken by the Lord
through the prophet, "Out of Egypt I have called my son."
When Herod saw that he had been tricked by the wise men,
he was infuriated, and he sent and killed all the children
in and around Bethlehem who were two years old or under,
according to the time that he had learned from the wise men.
Then was fulfilled what had been spoken through the prophet
Jeremiah: "A voice was heard in Ramah, wailing and loud
lamentation, Rachel weeping for her children; she refused to
be consoled, because they are no more."

—Matthew 2:13–18

The word providence, within the theological context, means God is in control and makes things happen for our good and God's glory. The late professor and theologian, Dr. E. Frank Tupper, has observed, "God's providence is sometimes scandalous." For example, when Jesus was born, Herod sent soldiers to kill the baby Jesus, believing that the newborn was a threat to his throne. In a dream, Joseph is warned about Herod's plan and escapes to Egypt with his family in tow. The scandal is that God did not provide the dream to all the Jewish families in Bethlehem. Boy babies and toddlers were slaughtered, and Matthew 2:18 records, "Rachel was weeping for her children and refused to be comforted."

We see the scandalous providence of God in the story of Plymouth Cannon. Although he escaped, he left behind his wife and their three children. To attribute his freedom to the providence of God begs the question, what about Cannon's wife and three children who were left behind to suffer in an evil, inhumane, and torturous institution? In what ways is God complicit?

Why do some people seem to be spared suffering and oppression while others are not?

Besides considering the unfairness of it all, what can you do to bring about a more just system where Blacks are lifted?

FACTS ABOUT BLACK OPPRESSION

Black Codes

During 1865 and 1866 they enacted the Black Codes as a system of social control that would be a substitute for slavery, fix the Negro in a subordinate place in the social order, and provide a manageable and inexpensive labor force. Blacks who were unemployed or without a permanent residence were declared vagrants. They could be arrested and fined and, if unable to pay, be bound out for terms of labor. States enacted careful provisions governing contracts between employer and laborer—in several states the words "master" and "servant" were freely used.

August Meier and Elliott Rudwick, *From Plantation to Ghetto*, 3rd ed. (New York: Hill and Wang, 1976), 170.

Day 19

Nancy said, "the very day before I escaped, I was required to go to his [her master's] bed-chamber to keep the flies off of him as he lay sick, or pretended to be so. Notwithstanding, in talking with me, he said that he was coming to my pallet that night, and with an oath he declared if I made a noise he would cut my throat. I told him I would not be there. Accordingly he did go to my room, but I had gone for shelter in another room. At this his wrath waxed terrible. Next morning I was called to account for getting out of his way, and I was beaten awfully." This outrage moved Nancy to a death-struggle for her freedom, and she succeeded by dressing herself in male attire.

—The True Story of Nancy Grantham

Jael came out to meet Sisera, and said to him, "Turn aside, my lord, turn aside to me; have no fear." So he turned aside to her into the tent, and she covered him with a rug. Then he said to her, "Please give me a little water to drink; for I am thirsty." So she opened a skin of milk and gave him a drink and covered him. He said to her, "Stand at the entrance of the tent, and if anybody comes and asks you, 'Is anyone here?' say, 'No.'" But Jael wife of Heber took a tent peg, and took a hammer in her hand, and went softly to him and drove the peg into his temple, until it went down into the ground—he was lying fast asleep from weariness—and he died. Then, as Barak came in pursuit of Sisera, Jael went out to meet him, and said to him, "Come, and I will show you the man whom you are seeking." So he went into her tent; and there was Sisera lying dead, with the tent peg in his temple.

—Judges 4:18–22

One of the great heroines of the Old Testament was a woman named Jael. Israel's Canaanite enemy, Sisera, had oppressed the chosen nation for years, stealing their crops and livestock. A woman named Deborah arose and mobilized an army led by a man named Barak and defeated Sisera and the Canaanites. However, Sisera was able to escape. He took refuge in the home of a woman named Jael, who deceived Sisera into thinking she was providing him sanctuary. After Jael won his confidence, Sisera fell asleep. While he slept, Jael took a tent peg and hammered it through his head.

Nancy Grantham's experience was similar to Jael's. To avoid being raped she, like many slaves, had to practice the art of deception. Upon realizing he had been deceived, Grantham's master beat her severely. This motivated her to even more deception as she planned her escape. Dressed in male attire, she ran away. She successfully eluded capture because the patrols were looking for a female. Many times, oppressed people are forced to engage in deceptive games in order to survive the evils of White supremacy.

In making reference to White supremacy, Wade Nobles, founding member of the Association of Black Psychologists, defines power as "the ability to define reality and to convince other people that it is their definition."[1] It is a fact that Nancy was deceptive; however, White supremacy teaches Blacks that being deceptive is noble when it is used to advance White hegemony, but when it is used to advance Black liberation the moralist will say it is wrong.

Nobles teaches us that part of the liberation for Black people is never to allow Whites to define their reality or determine what is right and wrong.

Where do you see White supremacy operating in your community or social circles?

How will you be a voice for the voiceless and stand up for what is right, just, and true?

Day 20

Isaac was twenty-two, quite black, and belonged to the "rising" young slaves of Delaware. He stated that he had been owned by a "blacksmith, a very hard man, by the name of Thomas Carper." Isaac was disgusted with his master's ignorance, and criticised him, in his crude way, to a considerable extent. . . . Both master and mistress were Methodists. . . . Sometimes Isaac would be called upon to receive correction from his master, which would generally be dealt out with a "chunk of wood" over his "no feeling" head. On a late occasion, when Isaac was being chunked beyond measure, he resisted, but the persistent blacksmith did not yield until he had so far disabled Isaac that he was rendered helpless for the next two weeks. While in this state he pledged himself to freedom and Canada, and resolved to win the prize by crossing the Bay.

— The True Story of Isaac White

Thus, the LORD says to my anointed, to Cyrus, . . . For the sake of my servant Jacob, and Israel my chosen, I call you by your name, I surname you, though you do not know me.

— Isaiah 45:1, 4

The most notable and frequently quoted phrase from the Declaration of Independence is "that all men are created equal," and that they have the right to "life, liberty and the pursuit of happiness." John Knox Witherspoon was one of the signers of the Declaration of Independence, yet he owned slaves. Witherspoon was not alone in this distinction, for other cosigners owned slaves as well. What makes Witherspoon distinctive is that he was the only college president and clergyman to sign.

In describing the cruel conditions from which he escaped, Isaac takes care to point out that the Carpers, the husband and wife who enslaved him, were Methodists. The common denominator between John Knox Witherspoon and Thomas Carper and his wife is that they professed to be Christians yet both subjugated other human beings to brutality by upholding the evil institution of Slavery.

Frederick Douglass wrote of this hypocrisy in his autobiography:

> Between the Christianity of this land, and the Christianity of Christ, I recognize the widest, possible difference—so wide, that to receive the one as good, pure, and holy, is of necessity to reject the other as bad, corrupt, and wicked. To be the friend of the one, is of necessity to be the enemy of the other. I love the pure, peaceable, and impartial Christianity of Christ: I therefore hate the corrupt, slaveholding, women-whipping, cradle-plundering, partial and hypocritical Christianity of this land. Indeed, I can see no reason, but the most deceitful one, for calling the religion of this land Christianity. I look upon it as the climax of all misnomers, the boldest of all frauds, and the grossest of all libels. Never was there a clearer case of "stealing the livery of the court of heaven to serve the devil in."[1]

In Isaiah 45, King Cyrus is God's agent of Jewish liberation from Babylonian captivity. He is even called God's messiah. God uses the king as an agent of liberation although Cyrus does not know God. In the struggle for justice, oppressed people must be open to whomever God sends for deliverance. Doctrinal alignment is not most essential, instead it is ethical alignment in the promotion of social justice. It is better to partner with a justice-committed atheist than to partner with a slave-owning Christian.

There are some American Descendants of Slavery who are seeking racial justice yet are self-proclaimed atheists. Are you willing to broaden your ethical alignment to unite in the work for racial justice with those who may not share your faith?

FACTS ABOUT BLACK OPPRESSION

Lynching

White vigilantes lynched an estimated four hundred black people across the South between 1868 and 1871. In rural Kentucky alone, white mobs lynched as many as two dozen African Americans each year between 1867 and 1871. Thirty-eight black people were lynched in South Carolina between the elections of 1870 and the spring of 1871. About thirty African Americans were killed in a single day in Meridian, Mississippi.

Henry Louis Gates Jr., *Stony the Road: Reconstruction, White Supremacy, and the Rise of Jim Crow* (New York: Penguin Press, 2019), 26

Day 21

Many reasons were given by Josephine for leaving the sunny South. She had a mistress, but was not satisfied with her—hadn't a particle of love for her; "She was all the time fussing and scolding, and never could be satisfied." She was very well off, and owned thirteen or fourteen head of slaves. She was a member of the Methodist Church, was stingy and very mean towards her slaves. Josephine, having lived with her all her life, professed to have a thorough knowledge of her ways and manners, and seemed disposed to speak truthfully of her. The name of her mistress was Eliza Hambleton, and she lived in Washington. Josephine had fully thought over the matter of her rights, so much so, that she was prompted to escape. So hard did she feel her lot to be, that she was compelled to resign her children, uncle and aunt to the cruel mercy of slavery. What became of the little ones, David, Ogden and Isaiah, is a mystery.

—The True Story of Josephine Robinson

So I returned, and considered all the oppressions that are done under the sun: and behold the tears of such as were oppressed, and they had no comforter; and on the side of their oppressors there was power; but they had no comforter.

—Ecclesiastes 4:1 KJV

Even after Emancipation, Blacks were the target of exclusion, intimidation, and oppression, supported by the federal and state legislatures, which were controlled by Whites, specifically White supremacists. Although Josephine Robinson professed to have no love for her oppressor, Eliza Hambleton, Robinson could not be considered a racist because she held no power to restrict Hambleton's liberties or economic advancements.

Blacks in America, by definition, cannot be racist. Racism is prejudice plus power. The writer of Ecclesiastes 4 says injustice exists because oppressors have power. Blacks may have prejudices against other groups including immigrants, but Blacks have no power to oppress and keep down other groups. Blacks do not control the government or the economic systems of this country that create laws and policies that deprive others of equal protection under the law. So, when Whites call prophets like Rev. Jeremiah Wright a "reverse racist," this merely highlights White ignorance on what racism is. Not only do Blacks not have power, but this has been our sad saga for 400 years. There has never been a law that Black people created that excluded any other group. Unfortunately, this has been the practice of White America against its Black brothers and sisters.

Even if you, as a White person, did not create structures that give you White skin advantage, you still benefit from it. How can you justify being Christian and benefit from structures that provide you with advantage at the expense of Black disadvantage?

Is it possible that Whites subconsciously know they have advantages and are quiet about racial injustice for fear they may lose them?

Day 22

For a year or more before setting out for freedom, Robert had watched his master pretty closely, and came to the conclusion, that he was "a monstrous blustery kind of a man; one of the old time fellows, very hard and rash — not fit to own a dog." He owned twelve slaves; Robert resolved that he would make one less in a short while. He laid the matter before his wife, "Sue," who was said to be the property of Susan Flinthrew, wife of John Flinthrew, of Cecil [C]ounty, Maryland. "Sue" having suffered severely, first from one and then another, sometimes from floggings, and at other times from hunger, and again from not being half clothed in cold weather, was prepared to consider any scheme that looked in the direction of speedy deliverance. The way that they were to travel, and the various points of danger to be passed on the road were fully considered; but Robert and Sue were united and agreed that they could not fare much worse than they had fared, should they be captured and carried back.

— The True Story of Robert Johns
and His Wife, Sue Ann

Then Jesus asked him, "What is your name?' He replied,
"My name is Legion; for we are many."

—*Mark 5:9*

New Testament scholar and systematic theology professor Dr. Obery Hendricks Jr. has noted, "When the demon-possessed man referred to himself as legion, he was using a military term." A legion was a Roman unit of three thousand to six thousand foot soldiers. Dr. Hendricks suggests to us that in casting out the legion of demons, Jesus was casting out the oppressive Roman Empire and sending them back across the sea. When the demons went into the water, Jesus was sending the Roman Empire, the source of this man's victimization, back across the sea.[1]

Sue Ann Johns was much like the demon-possessed man in Mark 5. Her suffering was due to systemic injustice and oppressive power. And just as the demon-possessed man could not be rendered healthy until his oppressor was annihilated, Sue Ann could never be delivered from her suffering until the demonic yoke of Slavery was cast into the sea.

How can you aid in the liberation of those who are experiencing systemic oppression today?

Day 23

Jacob was a stout and healthy-looking man, about twenty-seven years of age, with a countenance indicative of having no sympathy with Slavery. Being invited to tell his own story, describe his master, etc., he unhesitatingly relieved himself somewhat after this manner; "I escaped from a man by the name of Jesse W. Paten; he was a man of no business, except drinking whiskey, and farming. . . . I left because I didn't want to stay with him any longer. My master was about to be sold out this Fall, and I made up my mind that I did not want to be sold like a horse, the way they generally sold darkies then; so when I started I resolved to die sooner than I would be taken back. . . . I left my wife, and one child; the wife's name was Lear, and the child was called Alexander."

— The True Story of Jacob Blockson

"Woe to you, scribes and Pharisees, hypocrites! For you tithe mint, dill, and cumin, and have neglected the weightier matters of the law: justice and mercy and faith. It is these you ought to have practiced without neglecting the others."

—Matthew 23:23

Jesus condemned the Pharisees because their religion was a perfunctory collage of pretense and symbolism with no substance. He condemned them for tithing down to the mint leaf in their gardens but forgetting the more important things of religion: justice, mercy, and faith.

The enslaved were not helped through the ceremonial religious practices of their enslavers, but rather, relief would come only through the practice of the last three virtues that Jesus mentioned — justice, mercy, and faith.

Justice not only means releasing those held captive, but also providing them with reparations. Mercy means having a heart of empathy, and faith means being confident in God's abundance — not resorting to exploitation of the poor or hoarding wealth and resources. God is a God of abundance.

The reason why most enslaved were sold on the auction block was because they were a financial commodity of substantial value. Had slave owners like Jesse W. Paten exercised the faith of Matthew 23:23, they never would have put profit above people.

If we prioritize in our religion the things Jesus says to prioritize in Matthew 23:23, how would society look?

What would the response be to the 401 years of injustices committed against the American Descendants of Slavery?

What would be your response?

Day 24

"I 'scaped' from Sussex too, from a man by the name of George M. Davis, a large man, dark-complected, and about fifty years of age; he belonged to the old side Methodist Church, was a man with a family, and followed farming, or had farming done by me and others. Besides he was a justice of the peace. I always believed that the Master above had no wish for me to be held in bondage all my days; but I thought if I made up my mind to stay in Slavery, and not to make a desperate trial for my freedom, I would never have any better times. I had heard that my old mistress had willed me to her children, and children's children. I thought at this rate there was no use of holding on any longer for the good time to come, so here I said, I am going, if I died a trying."

— The True Story of George Alligood

"[F]or I was hungry and you gave me food, I was thirsty and you gave me something to drink, I was a stranger and you welcomed me, I was naked and you gave me clothing, I was sick and you took care of me, I was in prison and you visited me."

—Matthew 25:35–36

What makes bad people bad people is that they don't know they're bad people. And what makes good people good people is they don't realize they're good people. Jesus said in this famous parable that the bad people who were condemned asked Jesus, "'Lord, when was it that we saw you hungry or thirsty or a stranger or naked or sick or in prison, and did not take care of you?'" (Matt. 25:44). Jesus explained, "'just as you did not do it to one of the least of these, you did not do it to me" (v. 45).

The righteous were rewarded for doing good, yet they were totally unaware they were doing good. They asked, "When did we see you hungry, and naked, and in prison or sick?" Jesus replied, "What you have done to the least of these, you have done to me" (see vv. 37–40).

George Davis, who owned George Alligood, was a member of the Methodist church. He was unaware that by imposing brutality upon his slave he was imposing brutality upon Christ. He was unaware that every time he went to his Methodist church to worship God, he was persecuting God, who always identifies with the least. Davis likely found this out after he passed and there was a great separation.

Because Jesus closely identifies with the oppressed, if we apply the Matthew 25:35–36 principle to the racial injustices committed against Blacks in America today, Jesus is saying to us, "You've done it unto me." Thus, when we see Black males disproportionately jailed and sentenced, resulting in mass incarceration, yet remain silent, Jesus says, "You've done it unto me." When we see Blacks disproportionately dying from the coronavirus, yet remain silent, Jesus says, "You've done it unto me." When we see the George Floyds in the world being publicly lynched by a knee on the neck by police, yet remain silent, Jesus says, "You've done it unto me." When we see the economic divide with Whites at the top and Blacks, who built this country, at the bottom, yet remain silent, Jesus says, "You've done it unto me."

As we continue to see all these injustices committed against Blacks in America, and hear Jesus say "you've done it unto me," will you continue to remain silent?

FACTS ABOUT BLACK OPPRESSION

Reverse Redlining

Racially Discriminatory government activities did not end fifty years ago. On the contrary, some have continued into the twenty-first century. One of the more troubling has been the regulatory tolerance of banks' "reverse redlining"—excessive marketing of the exploitative loans in African American communities. This was an important cause of the 2008 financial collapse because these loans, called subprime mortgages, were bound to go into default. When they did, lower-middle-class African American neighborhoods were devastated, and their residents, with their homes foreclosed, were forced back into lower-income areas. In the early 2000s, reverse redlining was tolerated, sometimes winked at, by bank regulators.

Richard Rothstein, *The Color of Law: A Forgotten History of How Our Government Segregated America* (New York: Liveright Publishing, 2017), 109.

Day 25

"I came from Horse's Cross-Roads, not far from where my brother George came from. William Gray, rail road ticket agent at Bridgewater, professed to own me. He was a tolerable sized man, with very large whiskers, and dark hair; he was rather a steady kind of a man, he had a wife, but no child. The reason I left, I thought I had served Slavery long enough, as I had been treated none the best. I did not believe in working my life out just to support some body else. My master had as many hands and feet as I have, and is as able to work for his bread as I am; and I made up my mind that I wouldn't stay to be a slave under him any longer, but that I would go to Canada, and be my own master." James left his poor wife, and three children, slaves perhaps for life. The wife's name was Esther Ann, the children were called Mary, Henry, and Harriet. All belonged to Jesse Laten.

—The True Story of Jim Alligood

Woe to him who builds his house by unrighteousness, and his upper rooms by injustice; who makes his neighbors work for nothing, and does not give them their wages; who says, "I will build myself a spacious house with large upper rooms," and who cuts out windows for it, paneling it with cedar, and painting it with vermilion. Are you a king because you compete in cedar? Did not your father eat and drink and do justice and righteousness? Then it was well with him. He judged the cause of the poor and needy; then it was well. Is not this to know me? says the Lord. But your eyes and heart are only on your dishonest gain, for shedding innocent blood, and for practicing oppression and violence.

—Jeremiah 22:13–17

The reason Jim Alligood ran away from the cruel institution of Slavery was because "I did not believe in working my life out just to support somebody else." One of the reasons the prophet Jeremiah condemned King Jehoiakim was because he built his palace through exploitive labor. Rather, Jeremiah says, to give "justice . . . to the poor" (Jer. 22:16 NLT) is what it means to know God.

Slavery was the ultimate form of human exploitation and totally antithetical to the very nature of God.

Three words can define the Black experience in America. Blacks were exploited. Blacks were excluded. Blacks were eliminated. Prejudice did not produce Slavery. Slavery produced prejudice. In order to rationalize the exploitation of Black labor and the theft of Black wealth, Whites had to concoct pseudoscientific theories about the very nature of Black humanity. While Blacks were deemed to be three-fifths a person in the Constitution, it was highly believed that Black people were a subhuman species. There was a book, *The Negro a Beast*, by Charles Carroll, who argued that Blacks were not created in the image of God, but rather, when Genesis says, God created the beasts of the field, this is when Black people were created.[1]

Mehrsa Baradaran explains, "Blacks were 'articles of commerce,' as illustrated by the Constitution's three-fifths rule. Slave bodies were assets, credit, debt, currency—forms of capital and wealth. Between 1820 and the Civil War, banks across the South issued notes with images of slaves printed on the money. The currency of the South was the slave."[2]

Consequently, these pseudoscientific theories were simply created to justify the exploitation of Black labor and wealth in spite of this pernicious lie. The prophet Jeremiah condemns America with the words, "Woe to him who builds his house by unrighteousness, and his upper rooms by injustice."

Based on the history of this nation, and its treatment of enslaved, Jim-Crowed people, does America know God?

FACTS ABOUT BLACK OPPRESSION

Barriers to Wealth

The failure to grant ex-slaves an initial stake in American property ownership and the subsequent land taking from blacks has contributed to the comprehensive denial of black wealth accumulation. Apart from the barriers to landownership, black home ownership was restricted throughout the twentieth century by discriminatory redlining, differential access to government finance for home mortgages, and, most recently, by the subprime mortgage crisis induced by the banking system's loan-pushing schemes.

William A. Darity Jr. and A. Kirsten Mullen, *From Here to Equality: Reparations for Black Americans in the Twenty-First Century*, (Chapel Hill: University of North Carolina Press, 2020), 212.

Day 26

George Lewis had more years than any of his companions, being about forty years of age. He had been kept in as low a state of ignorance as the ingenuity of a slave-holder of Delaware could keep one possessed of as much mother-wit as he was, for he was not quite so ignorant as the interests of the system required. His physical make and mental capacity were good. He was decidedly averse to the peculiar institution in every particular. He stated, that a man named Samuel Laws had held him in bondage—that this "Laws was a man of no business—just sat about the house and went about from store to store and sat; that he was an old man, pretty grey, very long hair. He was a member of a church in the neighborhood, which was called Radical." Of this church and its members he could give but little account, either of their peculiarities or creed; he said, however, that they worshipped a good deal like the Methodists, and allowed their members to swear heartily for slavery.

— The True Story of George Lewis

"Not everyone who says to me, 'Lord, Lord,' will enter the kingdom of heaven, but only the one who does the will of my Father in heaven."

—Matthew 7:21

Enslaved people possessed an amazing degree of theological perception. George Lewis, without any seminary training, captured the essence of what the Christian faith is all about. The Christian faith can be summarized in one word—*practice*. Christianity as practice is designed to distinguish authentic Christianity from mere talk and theory. Of course, George Lewis was being facetious when he said, "They worshipped a good deal like the Methodists, and allowed their members to swear heartily for slavery."

Jesus' words in Matthew 7:21 make clear that holy words mean nothing without practice—obedience. The book of 1 John emphasizes the same thing:

> Little children, let no one deceive you. Everyone who does what is right is righteous, just as he is righteous.
>
> *(1 John 3:7)*

> Those who say, "I love God," and hate their brothers or sisters, are liars; for those who do not love a brother or sister whom they have seen, cannot love God whom they have not seen.
>
> *(1 John 4:20)*

Although the enslaved did not attend Bible college or seminary, they had keen spiritual insight into what constituted authentic Christian faith. And in contrast to the pretentious faith of the slave holders, the enslaved would simply sing, "Everybody talkin' 'bout heaven ain't going there."

In what ways have you demonstrated authentic Christian practice as it relates to advocating for economic justice on behalf of the American Descendants of Slavery?

In what ways can you expand your engagement?

Day 27

Sarah Mills set out for freedom long before she reached womanhood; being about sixteen years of age. She stated that she had been very cruelly treated, that she was owned by a man named Joseph O'Neil, "a tax collector and a very bad man." Under said O'Neil she had been required to chop wood, curry horses, work in the field like a man, and all one winter she had been compelled to go barefooted. Three weeks before Sarah fled, her mistress was called away by death; nevertheless Sarah could not forget how badly she had been treated by her while living. According to Sarah's testimony the mistress was no better than her husband. Sarah came from Boonsborough, near Hagerstown, Md., leaving her mother and other relatives in that neighborhood.

—The True Story of Sarah Mills

There is no longer Jew or Greek, there is no longer slave or free, there is no longer male and female; for all of you are one in Christ Jesus.

—Galatians 3:28

In *A Price for Their Pound of Flesh* by Daina Ramey Berry, the author catalogs the market value of enslaved human beings from infancy to senior adulthood. In many instances, women were valued as much as men, not simply for purposes of sexual exploitation, but also because they would be forced to work in the fields, as were enslaved men.

Sojourner Truth, in her famous speech "Ain't I a Woman?" echoes the sentiment of Sarah Mills, both complaining that they had to feel the sting of the lash and work in the field like a man. And that is why Sojourner Truth asked, "Ain't I a woman?"

The Apostle Paul's writing to the church at Galatia highlights the emancipatory nature of the gospel. In spite of the enslavers' attempt to make distinctions on who would be insiders and outsiders on the basis of race, Paul in his great baptismal creed declares that all people have insider status with God. The charismata does not discriminate on the basis of race. Paul proclaimed that in Christ there is no longer Jew or Greek, which is racial justice; or slave or free, which is economic justice; or male and female, which is gender justice.

Ibram X. Kendi, historian and author of *How to Be an Antiracist*, gives these terms: *racist, not racist, antiracist*. A racist is "one who is supporting racist policies through their actions or inaction or expresses a racist idea."[1] The not racist is someone who attempts not to make distinctions about people on the basis of race. The not racist will usually say, "I don't see color." Kendi espouses that "the color-blind individual, by ostensibly failing to see race, fails to see racism and falls into racist passivity."[2] According to Kendi, an antiracist is working aggressively to dismantle all systems and structures in society that make distinctions about people on the basis of race.[3]

A racist and a non-racist are quite similar in that neither is making a positive difference. The goal, then, should be to be an antiracist.

In what ways have you, at times, operated as a racist?

In what ways have you, at times, operated as a non-racist?

In what ways can you operate as an antiracist in the areas of law enforcement, the criminal justice system, government policy-making, at your place of employment, or in other social contexts?

FACTS ABOUT BLACK OPPRESSION

Reconstruction's Abrupt End

As the federal government signaled it would not interfere in the affairs of Southern states, and the Supreme Court overturned or defanged Reconstruction civil rights legislation, Southern Democrat lawmakers took the next logical step. . . . Virtually all of the former Confederate states threw out their Reconstruction-era constitutions—those that black people helped draft and which they voted to ratify—and wrote new ones that included disenfranchisement provisions, antimiscegenation provisions, and separate-but-equal Jim Crow provisions. Though "race neutral" in language, these new constitutions solidified Southern states as governed by legal segregation and discrimination.

Henry Louis Gates Jr., *Stony the Road: Reconstruction, White Supremacy, and the Rise of Jim Crow* (New York: Penguin Press, 2019), 34–35.

Day 28

"I am one of a family of sixteen; my mother and eleven sisters and brothers are now living; some have been sold to Alabama, and some to Tennessee, the rest are held in Richmond. My mother is now old, but is still in the service of Bailey. He promised to take care of her in her old age, and not compel her to labor, so she is only required to cook and wash for a dozen slaves. This they consider a great favor to the old 'grandmother.' It was only a year ago he cursed her and threatened her with a flogging. I left for nothing else but because I was dissatisfied with Slavery. The threats of my master caused me to reflect on the North and South. I had an idea that I was not to die in Slavery. I believed that God would assist me if I would try. I then made up my mind to put my case in the hands of God, and start for the Underground Rail Road."

—The True Story of Cornelius Henry Johnson

Now also when I am old and greyheaded, O God, forsake me not.

—Psalm 71:18 KJV

One can only imagine the sheer emotional torture that Cornelius Henry Johnson's mother must have felt knowing that her life would end in Slavery. It is customary for seniors to be given respect and homage, but Johnson's grandmother was threatened with a flogging and forced to work through old age. Our imagination can only wonder if she prayed Psalm 71:18, that at least God would not leave her when she's old and grey.

The tragedy for enslaved seniors was that the prayer for freedom was never answered on this side of heaven. If God did not answer this grandmother's prayer, does that not teach us that transactional prayers are not only unbiblical, but also not rooted in the Black religious experience? The greatest cause of atheism among Black Americans is White Christianity. Based on the transgenerational suffering of Black people, it is impossible to reconcile the Black experience with a God who answers prayer on demand.

Prayer for deliverance has gone unheard for Black America. In fact, a true student of history might argue that God answers the prayers of White racists. If the transactional view of prayer is truly what prayer is all about then we who are Christian should also be atheist because the transaction of God does not exist. However, the God who hates oppression and chooses to eradicate it through justice activism, the God who is on the side of the oppressed in their fight for justice and liberation, does exist.

How has your view of God changed?

What type of prayers should Christians pray in light of the fact that God does not always deliver suffering people from oppression?

Day 29

Stepney was an extraordinary man, his countenance indicating great goodness of heart, and his gratitude to his heavenly Father for his deliverance proved that he was fully aware of the Source whence his help had come. . . . Stepney was thirty-four years of age, tall, slender, and of a dark hue. He readily confessed that he fled from Mrs. Julia A. Mitchell, of Richmond; and testified that she was decidedly stingy and unkind, although a member of St. Paul's church. Still he was wholly free from acrimony, and even in recounting his sufferings was filled with charity towards his oppressors. He said, "I was moved to leave because I believed that I had a right to be a free man."

— The True Story of Stepney Brown

So if you think you are standing, watch out that you do not fall.

— 1 Corinthians 10:12

You may be surprised that Stepney Brown was not bitter toward Mrs. Mitchell or the others who enslaved him. The fact that he expressed charity toward his oppressors and was free from acrimony should not be interpreted as a spirit of docility. The fact that he escaped to freedom means he opposed the evil institution of Slavery. Instead of wasting emotional energy on his oppressor, he—like many slaves—played the game and channeled his emotional energies toward the pursuit of freedom.

Perhaps something deeper took place in Brown's spirit. Brown realized, like all spiritual geniuses, that some of the world's most horrendous evils are buried in the soil of everyone's heart. Given the proper circumstances they can bloom. That is why 1 Corinthians 10:12 says, "So if you think you are standing, watch out that you do not fall." God does not side with the oppressed because they are more noble than others; rather, God does so because they are more vulnerable than others. One of the privileges of being White in America is that you only have to live in a White world. While that does not prevent Whites from having struggles and interpersonal conflicts, one thing Whites do not have to do is to be judged by Black norms and standards. African Americans, on the other hand, must survive both in Black space and White space. Living in White space means having to live up to White norms and standards. It is critically important when Blacks are unable to do so that they guard their hearts and not take seriously how Whites may feel about them. Blacks must have power to disregard White America's evaluation of them, to guard their hearts with a sort of "ethnic armor." In other words, if Blacks allow the evil of White supremacy to enter their hearts, it becomes a psychological, emotional, and existential death sentence.

Has there been a time that you made a statement to a Black person unaware of the fact that what you said reinforced White supremacy and Black subordination?

Has anyone ever told you that your statement was insensitive? Were you in denial?

Were you a victim of White fragility?

Day 30

The appearance of these young mothers at first produced a sudden degree of pleasure, but their story of suffering quite as suddenly caused the most painful reflections. It was hardly possible to listen to their tales of outrage and wrong with composure. Both came from Kent [C]ounty, Maryland, and reported that they fled from a man by the name of Massey; a man of low stature, light-complexioned, with dark hair, dark eyes, and very quick temper; given to hard swearing as a common practice; also, that the said Massey had a wife . . . that, conjointly, Massey and his wife were in the habit of meting out cruel punishment to their slaves, without regard to age or sex, and that they themselves, (Anna Elizabeth and Sarah Jane), had received repeated scourgings at the hands of their master. Anna and Sarah were respectively twenty-four and twenty-five years of age; Anna was of dark chestnut color, while Sarah was two shades lighter; both had good manners, and a fair share of intelligence, which afforded a hopeful future for them in freedom. Each had a babe in her arms.

—The True Story of Anna Elizabeth Young
and Sarah Jane Bell

But Ruth said, "Do not press me to leave you or to turn back from following you! Where you go, I will go."

—Ruth 1:16

What is refreshing about Ruth and Naomi's relationship is that it is one of the few times, according to Old Testament scholar Renita Weems, that women are not in an acrimonious relationship. For example, Sarah and Hagar and Rachel and Leah turned on each other in the patriarchal society of the Bible to curry favor with males. But Ruth and Naomi created a bond of mutual support to overcome the hardship of famine in Moab and poverty and rape in Bethlehem. Renita Weems calls it "being just a sister away." Here are two women, Anna Elizabeth Young and Sarah Jane Bell, much like Ruth and Naomi, who bonded to overcome the Moab of Slavery, cruelty, and injustice.

Oppression often pits the oppressed against each other as they fight over limited resources. If the oppressed are to truly be free, the oppressed must discover the eternal strength to move from the selfishness of me to the solidarity of we. It is only when our race works together will we overcome White supremacy.

What type of trust did Anna Elizabeth and Sarah Jane have to have with each other to escape? For example, one could have turned on the other and then received potential freedom or some improved status.

In what ways does the White power structure pit Black people against each other?

Day 31

Robert Murray became troubled in mind about his freedom while living in Loudon [C]ounty, Virginia, under the heel of Eliza Brooks, a widow woman, who used him bad, according to his testimony. He had been "knocked about a good deal." A short while before he fled, he stated that he had been beat brutally, so much so that the idea of escape was beat into him. He had never before felt as if he dared hope to try to get out of bondage, but since then his mind had undergone such a sudden and powerful change, he began to feel that nothing could hold him in Virginia; the place became hateful to him. He looked upon a slave-holder as a kind of a living, walking, talking "Satan, going about as a roaring lion seeking whom he may destroy." He left his wife, with one child; her name was Nancy Jane, and the name of the offspring was Elizabeth. As Robert had possessed but rare privileges to visit his wife, he felt it less a trial to leave than if it had been otherwise. William Seedam owned the wife and child.

— The True Story of Robert Murray

Were you a slave when God called you? Well, never mind;
but if you have a chance to become free, use it. . . . God bought
you for a price; so do not become slaves of people.

—1 Corinthians 7:21, 23 GNT

These were two verses slave holders never read to their enslaved. It is apparent in verse 21 that Paul wanted to say something else but chose not to. We can only wonder what additional words Paul was going to say to enslaved people before he dismissed it with a "never mind."

Since the verse is leading toward the liberation of a slave, one could assume that Paul was going to give counsel to the enslaved on how they might resist their oppression. Perhaps Paul knew that his counsel would be unnecessary because, as in the case of Robert Murray, the brutality of Slavery beat the message of Paul into him.

Paul told the enslaved, "If you have an opportunity to get free, take it." Robert Murray took it. The great tragedy of his escape, however, is that he had to leave his wife and child behind in order to do it.

One of the reasons that many Black activists reject Christianity is because the Apostle Paul seems to be vague on issues of systemic injustice. This would make him out of alignment with organizations like Black Lives Matter and the American Descendants of Slavery. That is why the idea of the inerrancy of Scripture poses a serious problem for those who are oppressed. What you see in a text is often a reflection of your life situation. For those who claim that the Scripture is inerrant, the real dilemma is that there are no inerrant interpreters.

Why did Paul say "never mind"? Why couldn't he have said, "never Slavery"? When I said that Paul might have been leaning toward liberation, that is a reflection of my life situation as an American Descendant of Slavery, but

I must be honest enough to leave room for the idea that the Apostle Paul was taking a moderate position on Slavery. Does this invalidate the Bible for me? By no means! Because Paul is not Jesus.

What do you think Paul intended to say instead of "never mind"?

Does Paul's vagueness and potentially moderate view on Slavery negatively affect your view of the Christian faith?

How would you defend your faith, as a Christian, against those who say the Bible is a tool of Black oppression?

Day 32

Running away had been for a long time a favorite idea with Susan, as she had suffered much at the hands of different masters. The main cause of her flight was to keep from being sold again; for she had been recently threatened by Henry Harley, who "followed droving," and not being rich, at any time when he might be in want of money she felt that she might have to go. When a girl only twelve years of age, her young mind strongly revolted against being a slave, and at that youthful period she tried her fortune at running away. While she was never caught by her owners, she had the misfortune to fall into the hands of another slaveholder no better than her old master, indeed she thought that she found it even worse under him, so far as severe floggings were concerned. Susan was of a bright brown color, medium size, quick and active intellectually and physically, and although she had suffered much from Slavery, as she was not far advanced in years, she might still do something for herself. She left no near kin that she was aware of.

—The True Story of Susan Stewart

"Are not you Israelites the same to me as the Cushites?"
declares the LORD. "Did I not bring Israel up from Egypt,
the Philistines from Caphtor and the Arameans from Kir?"

—*Amos 9:7 NIV*

The prophet Amos reveals something that Black people should never forget: God loves Cushites as much as he loves Israelites. The Cushites are Black people. The word *cush* means "burnt face," and is another name used in the Bible for Africans. For Amos, a Jew, to say that God loves Black people as much as Israelites is revolutionary. Israel's status as God's chosen people was never a status given for the purpose of obtaining preferential treatment. Instead, it was a status for preferential service. God told Abraham in Genesis 12:3, "In you all the families of the earth shall be blessed."

For God to love Cushites as God loves the Israelites means that whatever God wanted for the Hebrew people God wants for Black people. It is apparent God wanted two things for the Hebrew people—liberation and self-determination through economic empowerment.

Susan Stewart perhaps never read Amos 9:7, but the words of Amos the prophet were in her heart and motivated her to flee from slavery, as the children of Israel did in the Old Testament. How liberating would it have been for the enslaved, and the early American Descendants of Slavery, for White Christians to affirm that God loves them as much as he loves Israel? Because White Christians profited from the exploited slave labor of Blacks, they had to embrace non-biblical, pseudoscientific theories about the humanity of Black people. These theories have never been fully extricated from the consciousness of the White church, which could, in fact, be called White-ianity or another form of White nationalism.

What would happen if White America were forced to embrace images of Jesus with the face of the lynched George Floyd?

How many White churches would close? How many White pastors would find themselves suddenly unemployed?

FACTS ABOUT BLACK OPPRESSION

Lynchings as Entertainment

The most horrifying subgenre of antiblack imagery—all too realistic—consisted of postcards of lynchings, which became ever more popular in the early years of the twentieth century. One example is "The Dogwood Tree," depicting five black bodies hanging from one tree in Sabine County, Texas, on June 22, 1908.

Henry Louis Gates Jr., *Stony the Road: Reconstruction, White Supremacy, and the Rise of Jim Crow* (New York: Penguin Press, 2019), 134.

Five states—Mississippi, Georgia, Texas, Alabama, and Louisiana—accounted for more than half of all lynchings in the nation. One of the most macabre formats for the murders was a spectacle lynching, which advertised the killing of a black person and provided special promotional trains to bring the audience, including women and children, to the slaughter.

Carol Anderson, *White Rage: The Unspoken Truth of Our Racial Divide* (New York: Bloomsbury, 2016), 43.

Day 33

Lewis' grey hairs signified that he had been for many years plodding under the yoke. He was about fifty years of age, well set, not tall, but he had about him the marks of a substantial laborer. He had been brought up on a farm under H. Lynch, whom Lewis described as "a mean man when drunk, and very severe on his slaves." The number that he ruled over as his property, was about twenty. Said Lewis, about two years ago, he shot a free man, and the man died about two hours afterwards; for this offence he was not even imprisoned. Lynch also tried to cut the throat of John Waters, and succeeded in making a frightful gash on his left shoulder (mark shown), which mark he will carry with him to the grave; for this he was not even sued. Lewis left five children in bondage, Horace, John, Georgiana, Louisa and Louis, Jr., owned by Bazil and John Benson.

—The True Story of Lewis Wilson

Meanwhile, standing near the cross of Jesus were his mother, and his mother's sister, Mary the wife of Clopas, and Mary Magdalene.

—John 19:25

H. Lynch's very name captures one of the horrors of the Black experience. At the end of the civil war up through the late 1950s, over 5,000 Black men and women were reportedly lynched. I say reportedly because nobody really knows how many lynched bodies are at the bottom of the Mississippi, Tallahassee, and Ohio Rivers. One of the most notorious lynchings was the lynching of Mary Turner of Augusta, Georgia, in 1918. She was nine months pregnant, and the White lynch mob tied her up, set her ablaze, ripped open her abdomen, and when the fetus came tumbling out alive, its cry was quickly hushed by one of the heels of the lynchers. Not one person was ever convicted for all of the lynchings that took place against Black Americans.[1] The purpose of lynching was not merely to kill the victims but to infuse fear and intimidation in the Black community to stay in the designated place assigned to them by White supremacy. The same could be said of H. Lynch, who shot and killed a free Black man with impunity.

In a sense, the execution of George Floyd was a lynching. The police officer, Derek Chauvin, was not simply killing George Floyd but sending a message to Black people who were seeking to save George Floyd's life. The message being: I can do whatever I want over Black bodies, and you are powerless to intervene — you must, like the Mother Mary, watch the crucifixion in agony and powerlessness.

When you reflect upon the death of George Floyd, what message do you think the police officers were attempting to send?

How did it affect those who watched it? In what ways is George Floyd a messianic figure?

Day 34

The fire of freedom obviously burned with no ordinary fervor in the breast of this slave mother, or she never would have ventured with the burden of seven children, to escape from the hell of Slavery. Ann Maria was about forty years of age, good-looking, pleasant countenance, and of a chestnut color, height medium, and intellect above the average. Her bearing was humble, as might have been expected, from the fact that she emerged from the lowest depths of Delaware Slavery. During the Fall prior to her escape, she lost her husband under most trying circumstances; he died in the poor-house, a raving maniac. Two of his children had been taken from their mother by her owner, as was usual with slave-holders, which preyed so severely on the poor father's mind that it drove him into a state of hopeless insanity. He was a "free man" in the eye of Delaware laws, yet he was not allowed to exercise the least authority over his children.

> — The True Story of Ann Maria Jackson
> and Her Seven Children — Mary Ann,
> William Henry, Frances Sabrina,
> Wilhelmina, John Edwin, Ebenezer Thomas,
> and William Albert

On hearing this, Jesus said to them, "It is not the healthy who need a doctor, but the sick."

—*Mark 2:17 NIV*

Yvette Carnell and Antonio Moore are cofounders of the American Descendants of Slavery (#ADOS movement), which is a grass-roots reparations movement. The #ADOS movement offers multiple suggestions on how American Descendants of Slavery might be recompensed for the injustices and atrocities committed against them. One of their proposals is to provide resources to address the mental illness that was caused by White oppression and Slavery. We should not be surprised that Ann Maria Jackson's husband died as a "raving maniac" and in a "state of hopeless insanity." We should be surprised, however, that not all Blacks, past and present, are in the same mental condition as Jackson's husband.

Injustice, plus powerlessness to change things, plus hopelessness that things will never change is what breeds mental illness among Black Americans (American Descendants of Slavery). Dr. Cornel West calls it nihilism—the belief that nothing makes sense and it never will. I see this sense of hopelessness and despair being expressed in the cities of America through riots and civil unrest due to the execution of George Floyd by the Minneapolis Police.

Many times, Blacks hear Whites say, "I am color-blind." First of all, Blacks already know such a statement is not true. It seems apparent that Whites are not color-blind but are very color conscious. The idea of being color-blind is not only an illusion but is also unhealthy. Whenever you say to a Black person, "I see all people alike," it ignores the fact that all people's experiences based on race are not alike. For example, when Whites say, "all lives matter," to counter the affirmation that "Black lives matter," it is a subtle attempt to dismiss the uniqueness of Black suffering and pain.

To say Black lives matter is not implying that White lives don't matter. That does not have to be stated because of all the privileges and advantages that America gives to White life. Jesus said, "People who are well do not need a doctor, but those who are sick." The religion of Jesus Christ is one that seeks to heal those who have been broken by oppressive systems physically, socially, economically, and mentally.

Those who believe in critical race theory believe that racism cannot be retracted in the United States. To quote Professor Derrick Bell, "Black people will always be the faces at the bottom of the well." How do you respond to the critical race theorists? What gives you hope that there is hope?

Day 35

Sam Archer was to "become free at thirty-five years of age." He had already served thirty years of this time; five years longer seemed an age to him. The dangers from other sources presented also a frightful aspect. Sam had seen too many who had stood exactly in the same relations to Slavery and freedom, and not a few were held over their time, or cheated out of their freedom altogether. He stated that his own mother was "kept over her time," simply "that her master might get all her children." Two boys and two girls were thus gained, and were slaves for life. These facts tended to increase Sam's desire to get away before his time was out; he, therefore, decided to get off via the Underground Rail Road.

—The True Story of Sam Archer

But do not ignore this one fact, beloved, that with the Lord one day is like a thousand years, and a thousand years are like one day. The Lord is not slow about his promise, as some think of slowness, but is patient with you, not wanting any to perish, but all to come to repentance.

—2 Peter 3:8–9

Many of Paul's writings in the New Testament were used to justify the institution of Slavery. For example, Colossians 3:22 reads, "slaves obey your human masters in all things, not only when they are watching you because you want to gain their approval; but do it with a sincere heart because of your reverence for the Lord" (GNT).

While there are scholars who believe that Paul is not the author of Colossians, it still is a part of canon Scripture, and we may wonder why the Apostle Paul, who told the enslaved to escape in 1 Corinthians 7:21, also told them, in multiple other epistles, to obey their masters. The answer is found in the early Christian's belief in the imminent return of Christ, what is known as the Parousia, which means appearing.

The early Christians believed that the time between Christ's ascension and second coming would take place in their lifetime. Jesus alluded to this in Mark 13:1–2. Second Peter seeks to explain the delay of the Parousia by suggesting that God does not view time as we do. He explains, "A day is like a thousand years with God." He further states that the delay was to give people time to change before the judgment. Had Christ come in the first century, his kingdom would have eradicated Slavery and all social injustice.

Thankfully, Sam Archer did not wait until the return of Christ before he sought to escape Slavery through the Underground Railroad. In fact, his very act in defiance of Slavery was a precursor and dress rehearsal to the second coming of Christ. What Archer did as an individual, Christ will do for the collective.

Do you think there are present-day policies or laws that need to be eradicated or changed in order to bring justice for ADOS?

How can you actively support the redress of ADOS justice concerns without proposing "waiting until a better time" as the solution?

Day 36

The father of this family was sixty-five years of age, and his working days were apparently well nigh completed. The mother was fifty-seven years of age; son twenty-seven; daughters seventeen and fifteen years of age. The old man was smart for his years, but bore evidence that much hard labor had been wrung out of him by Slavery. Diana said that she had been the mother of twelve children; five had escaped to Canada, three were in their graves, and three accompanied her; one was left in Maryland. They had seen hard times, according to the testimony of the old man and his companion, especially under David Snively, who, however, had been "removed by the Lord" a number of years prior to their escape; but the change proved no advantage to them, as they found Slavery no better under their mistress, the widow, than under their master. . . . The belief was pretty generally entertained with the slaves that the slaveholder would have to answer for his evil doings in another world.

> —The True Story of Jerry Mills and Wife, Diana, Son, Cornelius and Two Daughters, Margaret, and Susan

"But Abraham replied, 'Son, remember that in your lifetime you received your good things, while Lazarus received bad things, but now he is comforted here and you are in agony.'"

—*Luke 16:25 NIV*

The predecessor to Dr. Martin Luther King Jr. at the Dexter Avenue Baptist Church in Montgomery, Alabama, was the very brilliant and eccentric Rev. Vernon Johns. He often would offend the Black professional class of the church by selling watermelons and other produce on the church's front lawn after worship. His intent was to encourage Blacks to be producers and not consumers and clients of White America.

Despite his idiosyncrasies, however, his parishioners, many of whom were professors at Alabama State University, could not question his brilliance. On one occasion, Rev. Johns, in condemnation of Montgomery's segregationist policies, preached a sermon entitled "Segregation in the Next Life." It is the story of the rich man and Lazarus, who wanted only the crumbs that fell from the rich man's table.

Rev. Vernon Johns highlights the fact that when both died and went into the next life, there is a great reversal. The poor man is enjoying the eschatological banquet in the presence of Abraham while the rich man is in torment in hell.

Even from the pit of hell, the rich man could not get out of his mindset that certain people were created to serve him. Abraham explained to him that there was a great reversal: those who experienced deprivation while on earth would experience heavenly bounty, while those who experienced temporal bounty would experience deprivation in the next life.

Jerry Mills and his fellow laborers were on target in their eschatological viewpoint that "the slaveholder would have to answer for his evil doings in another world."

No wonder one of the freedom songs of the Civil Rights Movement was, "I'm gonna sit at the welcome table one of these days, I'm gonna tell God how you treated me one of these days."[1]

Like Vernon Johns, what demonstrative act can you make to encourage economic or social justice, or community uplift, for the poor and specifically for the American Descendants of Slavery?

FACTS ABOUT BLACK OPPRESSION

White Monopoly of Power

According to DiAngelo's data on America's institutions in 2016–2017, Whites have a monopoly on the decision-making powers in America's strongest institutions:

— Ten richest Americans: 100 percent White (several of whom are among the ten richest in the world)
— US Congress: 90 percent White
— US governors: 96 percent White
— Top military advisors: 100 percent White
— President and vice president: 100 percent White
— US Home Freedom Caucus: 99 percent White
— Current US presidential cabinet: 91 percent White
— People who decide which TV shows we see: 93 percent White
— People who decide which books we read: 90 percent White
— People who decide which news is covered: 85 percent White
— People who decide which music is produced: 95 percent White
— People who directed the one hundred top-grossing films of all time, worldwide: 95 percent White
— Teachers: 82 percent White
— Full-time college professors: 84 percent White
— Owners of men's professional football teams: 97 percent White

Robin DiAngelo, *White Fragility: Why It's So Hard for White People to Talk About Racism* (Boston: Beacon Press, 2018), 31.

Day 37

As a slave, subjected to the whims and passions of his master, Henry made up his mind that he could not stand it longer. The man who mastered it over him was called Nathaniel Dixon, and lived in Somerset Co., near Newtown. This Dixon was not content with his right to flog and abuse Henry as he saw fit, but he threatened to sell him, as he would sell a hog. At this time Henry was about twenty-four years of age, but a man of more substantial parts physically was rarely to be seen. Courage was one of his prominent traits. This threat only served to arouse him completely. . . . Slavery he considered as death to him; and since his master had threatened him, he looked upon him as his greatest enemy, and rather than continue a slave he preferred living in the swamps with wild animals.

— The True Story of Henry Cotton

"And at his gate lay a poor man named Lazarus, covered with sores, who longed to satisfy his hunger with what fell from the rich man's table; even the dogs would come and lick his sores."

—Luke 16:20–21

The name Lazarus literally means *God helps*; however, when you look at the wretched condition of his life, Lazarus's reality does not reflect his name. He was houseless, hungry, sick, and forgotten. He was considered nonhuman in the eyes of Devis, which means rich man. We are told in verse 21 that the dogs licked his sores. At first glance, that may appear to be gross and unsanitary; however, Luke is telling us that dogs had more compassion on human pain than the privileged. The dogs' saliva was used by the animals for medicinal purposes.

No wonder Henry Cotton preferred to live in the swamps with wild animals than to continue his life being enslaved. The utter moral depravity of enslavers yielded them a level of compassion that was less than that of a predatory wild animal.

Although Black people are 13 percent of the population in America, they represent a disproportionate number of houseless, homeless people. Men, women, and children live outdoors clutching each other for warmth against the biting chill of winter nights. They are forced to live in shelter houses where there is always a threat of violence, disease, bed bugs, and now coronavirus. Like the swamps in which Henry Cotton lived, the streets today may show more compassion than the White privileged class.

In the story of Lazarus and Devis, Devis did not go to hell because he did something to Lazarus. He went to hell because he did nothing—he did not do anything to improve Lazarus's state.

Based on the message of this story, is the White church in America going to hell?

Day 38

In the sale of her children, Cordelia was a little regarded as if she had been a cow. "I felt wretched," she said, with emphasis, "when I heard that Nancy had been sold," which was not until after she had been removed. "But," she continued, "I was not at liberty to make my grief known to a single white soul. I wept and couldn't help it." But remembering that she was liable, "on the first insult," to be sold herself, she sought no sympathy from her mistress, whom she describes as "a woman who shows as little kindness towards her servants as any woman in the States of America. She neither likes to feed nor clothe well." With regard to flogging, however, in days past, she had been up to the mark. "A many a slap and blow" had Cordelia received since she arrived at womanhood, directly from the madam's own hand.

—The True Story of Cordelia Loney

The word of the LORD came to me: Mortal, with one blow I am about to take away from you the delight of your eyes; yet you shall not mourn or weep, nor shall your tears run down.

—Ezekiel 24:15–16

To highlight the suffering that Jerusalem would experience with the invasion of the Babylonians, God used an experience in the life of Ezekiel to illustrate how unbearable the pain would be. Ezekiel was told that his wife, whom he passionately loved, would die of a stroke. Ezekiel was told that when it happens, he was not to mourn or cry.

This command not to mourn and cry was not normal, natural, or healthy. God designed human beings with tear ducts to serve as emotional release valves during times of grief.

Ezekiel was forbidden to grieve to highlight how God would not show sympathy for Jerusalem's sins when the Babylonians came and destroyed their temple and their entire civilization.

Like Ezekiel, Cordelia Loney was not at liberty to make her grief known to a single White soul. As she watched the sale of her children, she had to maintain Ezekiel-like stoicism toward an atrocity that was ripping her heart out.

Even today, White America feels very uncomfortable with Black people expressing their rage and grief toward centuries of inhumane treatment. Robin DiAngelo refers to it as *White Fragility* in her book by the same name. She explains the term as being the inability of White people to be confronted with the reality of Black pain and suffering.[1] What God commanded Ezekiel to do was neither normal nor healthy. Jesus said, "Blessed are they that mourn," and Black people have a deep well of atrocities and injustice to mourn.

Most Blacks suffer in silence. How can you go beyond your comfort zone to learn firsthand about the oppression and pain inflicted on the masses of present-day American Descendants of Slavery in your local community/city?

Day 39

He declared that he fled because his owner wanted "to work him hard without allowing him any chance, and had treated him rough." Frederick was also one of Mr. Bockover's chattels; he left his wife, Elizabeth, with four children in bondage. They were living in Eatontown, North Carolina. It had been almost one year since he had seen them. Had he remained in Norfolk he had not the slightest prospect of being reunited to his wife and children, as he had been already separated from them for about three years. This painful state of affairs only increased his desire to leave those who were brutal enough to make such havoc in his domestic relations.

—The True Story of Frederick Nixon

[M]ake it your ambition to lead a quiet life: You should mind your own business and work with your hands, just as we told you.

—1 Thessalonians 4:11 NIV

What a powerful purpose the Apostle Paul is calling Christians to live out! He calls upon Christians to have ambition. Author Frederick C. Van Tatenhove, in *Ambition: Friend or Enemy*, writes, "Ambition is defined as energy expressed in active behaviors towards some purpose or aspiration."[1]

Ambition is part of our native human cargo. Paul not only applauds ambition, but he also gives us specifics on what we should be ambitious toward. Living a quiet life means to be a good citizen. Minding your own business means developing something of your own. Working with your hands means agricultural work. No other verse captures the ambition of the enslaved community like 1 Thessalonians 4:11.

Frederick Nixon ran away from Mr. Bockover because he sought to destroy Nixon's God-planted ambition. This despotic enslaver aimed "to work him hard without allowing him any chance."

In the parable of the Prodigal Son, the hogs were never discontent in the hog pen, but the prodigal son knew he did not belong there. He had ambitions beyond living among swine because the prodigal was of a higher heredity than the hogs. He knew that he was made in the image of his father.

The reason why humans have ambition beyond being "Mr. Bockover's chattels" is because to be made in the image of God means to have ambition beyond animal status. Perhaps the greatest crime committed against Black people in America is that Slavery aborted Black ambitions and aspirations. One of the cruelest punishments inflicted upon people during the Spanish inquisition was to put people in rooms where the ceiling was low and they could not fully stand up. They had to always be bent over. They could not rise to their full stature. Likewise, in a sense, there is an invisible ceiling on Black people. Regardless of the ambition and skill set, there is an invisible ceiling that all Black people are aware of that prohibits us from rising to our full stature. Dr. Martin Luther King Jr. said that the civil rights struggle enabled Black people to raise their backs up because no one can ride your back unless it's bent.

Still today, the dreams and aspirations of many American Descendants of Slavery have been aborted because of oppression and poverty. How can you make a difference?

Day 40

The first arrival to be here noticed consisted of David Bennett, and his wife Martha, with their two children, a little boy named George, and a nameless babe one month old. . . . David, the husband, had been in bonds under Captain James Taylor. Martha, the wife, and her two children were owned by George Carter. Martha's master was represented as a very barbarous and cruel man to the slaves. He made a common practice of flogging females when stripped naked. This was the emphatic testimony of Martha. Martha declared that she had been so stripped, and flogged by him after marriage. . . . During the painful interview the mind would involuntarily picture this demon, only as the representative of thousands in the South using the same relentless sway over men and women; and this fleeing victim and her little ones, before escaping, only as sharers of a common lot with many other mothers and children, whose backs were daily subjected to the lash.

> —The True Story of David Bennett, His Wife, Martha, and Their Two Children

Then Pilate had Jesus flogged with a lead-tipped whip. The soldiers wove a crown of thorns and put it on his head, and they put a purple robe on him. "Hail! King of the Jews!" they mocked, as they slapped him across the face.

—*John 19:1–3 NLT*

It is apparent from John's Gospel that the Roman governor Pilate did not want to sign Jesus' death warrant, despite the mob's insistence. Pilate employed every maneuver to avoid Jesus' crucifixion yet satisfy the mob's hunger for Jesus' death. Pilate had Jesus flogged. Flogging was practically considered a form of capital punishment in and of itself. The *New Living Translation* described the flagrum used in the flogging as an instrument with a lead-tipped whip.

The trauma of the flogging experience was enough to kill Jesus even without crucifixion. Jesus died before the other malefactors who were crucified beside him because Jesus was already near the point of death because of the flogging.

What Martha endured under the bondage of Captain James Taylor is reminiscent of Jesus' crucifixion. The plantations of the Old South were nothing less than horror and torture chambers for the Black enslaved—a "Good Friday" every day.

It is the role of the church to identify with the whipped Savior and not with the empire. The names of empires change but their thirst for power and domination is what ties them together throughout the annals of time. There is always a great temptation to put the flag above the cross and to make Jesus a mascot of the American empire. As this Lent of Liberation draws to a close, let us remember that the Christian's ultimate patriotism is not to empire but the kingdom of God; and we pray, "Thy Kingdom come on earth as it is in Heaven." We look forward to the day when the kingdoms of this world shall become the kingdoms of our Lord and the Christ, and he shall reign forever; and his dominion shall be without end (Rev. 11:15).

Is your loyalty to God's kingdom or the American empire?

How will that loyalty affect the way you live?

Seeing that the ultimate goal of the Black struggle for liberation is reparations, would you be willing to have your taxes increased in order to finally fix America's 400-year racial injustice against Black people?

Will you be a vocal advocate for reparations for the American Descendants of Slavery?

Appendix

The tentacles of generational poverty and oppression for the masses of American Descendants of Slavery reach all the way back to 1619. While other groups that have been harmed by the laws, policies, and practices of the United States government have received redress, the American Descendants of Slavery, who actually built the country and who have been the victims of state-sponsored terrorism for 401 years, have not been made whole. For example, Native Americans received reparations for the U.S. seizure of their land, Jews received reparations from the U.S. for the Holocaust,[1] and Japanese Americans received reparations in 1988 for Japanese internment during World War II.[2]

The knowledge of truth demands a response.

The just response is to advocate for reparations for the American Descendants of Slavery. #ADOS cofounders Yvette Carnell and Antonio Moore, through extensive investigative research and consultation, have outlined a Black Agenda which seeks redress for American Descendants of Slavery for centuries of targeted oppression and neglect by the United States government. "Without these measures being instituted," Moore says in the agenda, "ADOS are locked out of the country our ancestors built during chattel slavery. Without reforms through transformative government, we will be left to continue living a third-world life in a first-world country."

The truth of ADOS life is seen nowhere more clearly than the racial wealth gap in this country:

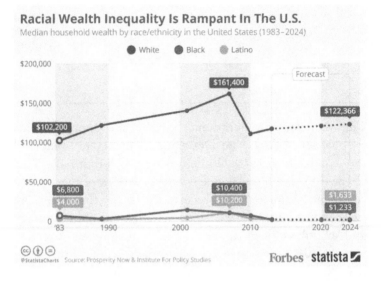

Racial Wealth Inequality Is Rampant In The U.S.
Median household wealth by race/ethnicity in the United States (1983–2024)

White   Black   Latino

$200,000

$161,400

Forecast

$150,000

$122,366

$102,200

$100,000

$50,000

$6,800
$4,000

$10,400
$10,200

$1,633
$1,233

0

'83   1990   2000   2010   2020   2024

@StatistaCharts   Source: Prosperity Now & Institute For Policy Studies

Forbes statista

That is why the agenda developed by Carnell and Moore outlines specific policy measures for all Blacks, with reparations designated specifically for ADOS, that should be adopted to pay the debt America owes to American Descendants of Slavery. In the book of James, as Christians, we are challenged to be a doer of God's word and not a hearer only. The Black Agenda is a bridge that allows you to move from a passive learner to an active participant and ally in supporting the racial justice work of the American Descendants of Slavery.

BLACK AGENDA

As a specific group with a specific justice claim, the #ADOS movement demands a specific agenda with policy prescriptions that address the losses stemming from the institution of slavery, Jim Crow, redlining, convict leasing, mass incarceration and immigration.

We demand a New Deal for Black America which includes, but is not limited to:

— We need set asides for American descendants of slavery, not "minorities," a throw-away category which includes all groups except white men. That categorization has allowed Democrats to use programs like affirmative actions as "giveaways" to all groups in exchange for votes. The bribery must end. That begins with a new designation on the Census with ADOS and another for Black immigrants. Black immigrants should be barred from accessing affirmative action and other set asides intended for ADOS, as should Asians, Latinos, white women, and other "minority" groups. In addition, ADOS hiring and employment data must be demanded for all businesses receiving tax credits, incentives, and governmental support. As well as all governmental agencies national, state and local. It is our belief that this will show that there are minimal if any ADOS professionals in fields including but not limited to engineering, medical, legal and tech.

— Once affirmative action is streamlined as a government program only and specifically for ADOS, the program should be fully reinstituted.

— The Supreme Court decided wrongly when it gutted the Voting Rights Act. As the Atlanta Journal Constitution

Reprinted courtesy of American Descendants of Slavery (https://ados101.com /black-agenda).

article "It's Time to Solve the Mystery of the 100,000 Mystery Votes" indicates, the protections outlined in the Voting Rights Act are essential to protecting the rights of ADOS in America. Reinstituting the protections of The Voting Rights Act is a key part of our agenda.

— Black businesses only received 1.7% of the $23.09 billion in total SBA loans under President Obama's SBA (Small Business Administration), after having previously received 8.2% under President George W. Bush. Succeeding as an entrepreneur requires capital, so our agenda demands that 15% of SBA loans be distributed to ADOS businesses.

— We seek a multi-billion dollar infrastructure plan targeted to ADOS communities, including, but not limited to, the Black Belt, Flint, Michigan. A Reuters examination published in 2016 found 3,000 cities with poisoning rates higher than Flint.

— Residents of majority ADOS areas that have been poisoned under the federal, local and state government's watch, such as not only Flint, Michigan, but Denmark, South Carolina, and others, must be financially compensated for the benign neglect of the Environmental Protection Agency and the government in general. The Justice Department must also institute protections which exact heavy fines and federal criminal prosecution for future offenders.

— Mass incarceration has wreaked havoc on Black American families. By some accounts there are literally more black males imprisoned than all women are incarcerated on the planet. To give context there are 20 million black males, and they largely descend from slavery. While there are 4 billion women globally, both groups producing the same number of incarcerated. The reinvention of slavery through use of the 13th Amendment is chronicled by Douglas Blackmon in his PBS documentary "Slavery by Another Name", it is our position this must be corrected. We demand an immediate assessment of the numbers of the #ADOS prison populations at the state and federal level. We also demand that there be review if punishment (bail amounts, sentence lengths, amount of time served before parole) is being levied at unfairly high levels on #ADOS based on gender and race for similar crimes to other groups. We demand that there be real prison reform in the form of investment into counseling, job training, and rehabilitation for our incarcerated.

— In the early eighties America committed to "strengthen the capacity of historically Black colleges and universities to provide quality education" in Executive Order 12320. President Obama undermined that commitment with changes to the PLUS Loan requirements. We call for legislation to triple the current federal allotment to HBCUs. Schools like Georgetown, built by slaves, have an endowment of over a billion dollars. This is a transfer of wealth from ADOS to whites. Our agenda demands that the federal government fully endow our remaining HBCUs in a dollar amount that meets the budgetary needs of each institution. In addition, ADOS students who attend HBCUs should receive a discount in the form of a 75 percent tax credit, given that our inability to pay the rising cost of education is directly tied to the racial wealth gap coming from slavery. ADOS who choose schools outside of the HBCU network should receive a 50 percent government funded credit.

— Findings published in *USA Today* concluded that top universities graduate ADOS in tech, but those graduates can't find jobs in Silicon Valley. Only 2% of technology workers at seven Silicon Valley companies are Black, according to the report, and many of those are Black immigrants, not ADOS. And according to a study by Rutgers Professor Hal Salzman, American colleges graduate more tech workers than tech companies need, hence the H1-B program reduces opportunities for ADOS searching for careers in technology. The government must strictly limit the number of H1-B Visa workers tech companies that flow in each year.

— Audit the banks to see if there are patterns of racial discrimination in lending, and require these banks to extend loans to ADOS businesses. These banks received bailout from taxpayers and owe a debt to all taxpayers, regardless of race. In addition, banks such as Wells Fargo used predatory schemes historically, not just during the Great Recession, to eviscerate Black Wealth. Lending to Black businesses and institutions would be a beginning for banks to redress the harm they've caused to the ADOS community.

— Mandate that the government's advertising budget include Black media. There is no ADOS community without our own media. Incentivize through legislative action that all major companies spend 10% of their advertising budget with ADOS media in exchange for tax credits. In addition, mandate that 10% of government advertising for governmental agencies, armed forces and other ancillary programs go to majority ADOS owned media companies.

— ADOS college debt should be forgiven in the same way losses were forgiven for the banks on Wall Street. Those executives oversaw the evaporation of billions in global wealth. ADOS graduates bought into the idea that the key to success in life was an education, and there was a place for us in America, only to find after graduation that we were locked out. We can't afford to bear the burden of a lie.

— A health care credit to pay for medical coverage for all ADOS. This would cover surgery, pharmaceutical, and counseling needs. As an example we would like to see a Lineage Therapy, whereby #ADOS leadership, in co-operation with licensed therapists and psychiatrists, develop a therapy curriculum to help members of the ADOS understand and manage their ancestral traumas. This therapy should come at no cost to the ADOS community.

— America has never atoned for its original sin of slavery in the form of reparations. It is our position that H.R. 40 be fully rewritten to include reference to ADOS as the recipient group, cash payments, and additional supportive measures implemented. We need to gather the data on the level of wealth that was lost as a direct result of slavery, and the era of Jim Crow that followed. The paper "The Economics of Reparations" assessed the value today as:

> Professor Sandy Darity Jr. — a leading economist and premiere scholar in the area of American reparations — and Dania Frank have illustrated using the work of Vedder, Gallaway and Klingaman, the gains in wealth to white southerners from ownership of blacks in 1859 was $3.2 million. In today's dollars, the value of that debt is estimated to be somewhere between $5 to $10 trillion dollars, depending upon the interest rate used for compounding purposes.

#ADOS demands that there be a real review of direct payouts needed to be made to eligible recipients from gathered data, and progress be made toward making #ADOS families whole.

Without these measures being instituted, ADOS are locked out of the country our ancestors built during chattel slavery. Without reforms through transformative government, we will be left to continue living a third world life in a first world country.

Notes

INTRODUCTION

1. Molefi Kete Asante, *The African American People: A Global History* (New York: Routledge, 2012), 41–42.
2. Liz Mineo, "Tanner Lecturer Stevenson Seeks a National Conversation about Slavery's Legacy," *The Harvard Gazette*, December 7, 2017. Accessed June 16, 2020. https://news.harvard.edu/gazette/story/2017/12/bryan-stevenson-seeks-national-conversation-about-slaverys-legacy/.
3. Martin Luther King Jr., *Where Do We Go from Here: Chaos or Community* (Boston: Beacon Press, 1967), 90.
4. William Still, *The Underground Railroad: A Record* (Philadelphia: People's Publishing Company, 1871).
5. Cheri L. Mills, *The Angela Project Presents the 400th Year Commemoration Ceremony: 1619–2019: Commemorating 400 Years of Institutionalized Slavery in Colonized America* (Louisville, KY: Simmons College of Kentucky Press, 2019).

DAY 2

1. James Washington, *A Testament of Hope* (San Francisco: Harper Collins, 1991), 292.
2. Frederick Douglass, "Frederick Douglass Declares There Is 'No Progress without Struggle,'" *HERB: Resources for Teachers*, https://herb.ashp.cuny.edu/items/show/1245.
3. "MLK: A Riot Is the Language of the Unheard," *60 Minutes*, August 25, 2013, https://www.cbsnews.com/news/mlk-a-riot-is-the-language-of-the-unheard/.

DAY 3

1. Henry Louis Gates Jr., *Stony the Road: Reconstruction, White Supremacy, and the Rise of Jim Crow* (New York: Penguin Press, 2019), 60–61.

DAY 4

1. Michelle Alexander, *The New Jim Crow: Mass Incarceration in the Age of Colorbindness* (New York: The New Press, 2012), 6–7.

DAY 6

1. "No Hiding Place," Hymnary.org, https://hymnary.org/text/went_to_the _rocks_for_to_hide_my_face.

DAY 7

1. Jeffrey Robert Young, "Slavery in Antebellum Georgia," in *New Georgia Encyclopedia*, October 20, 2003. Last modified July 26, 2017. https://www.georgiaencyclopedia.org/articles/history-archaeology /slavery-antebellum-georgia.
2. William A. Darity Jr. and A. Kirsten Mullen, *From Here to Equality: Reparations for Black Americans in the Twenty-First Century* (Chapel Hill: University of North Carolina Press, 2020), 278.

DAY 9

1. Stephanie E. Jones-Rogers, *They Were Her Property: White Women as Slave Owners in the American South* (New Haven, CT: Yale University Press, 2019), ebook, 42, 88.
2. Erica Armstrong Dunbar, *Never Caught: The Washingtons' Relentless Pursuit of Their Runaway Slave, Ona Judge* (New York: 37 Ink/Atria, 2017).

DAY 10

1. Mehrsa Baradaran, *The Color of Money: Black Banks and the Racial Wealth Gap* (Cambridge, MA: Belknap Press of Harvard University Press, 2017), 10.

DAY 12

1. Robert M. Franklin, *Crisis in the Village* (Minneapolis: Fortress Press, 2007), 175.
2. Kriston McIntosh, Emily Moss, Ryan Nunn and Jay Shambaugh, "Examining the Black-White Wealth Gap," Brookings, February 7, 2020, https://www.brookings.edu/blog/up-front/2020/02/27/examining-the -black-white-wealth-gap/.

DAY 17

1. Darity and Mullen, *From Here to Equality*, 231.

DAY 19

1. "Quotes about Power," White Allies in Training, October 23, 2015, https://whitealliesintraining.com/201 5/10/03/quotes-about-power/.

DAY 20

1. Frederick Douglass, *The Narrative of the Life of Frederick Douglass* (London: Arcturus, 2018), 163–64.

DAY 22

1. Obery M. Hendricks Jr., *The Politics of Jesus: Rediscovering the True Revolutionary Nature of Jesus' Teachings and How They Have Been Corrupted* (repr., New York: Three Leaves, 2007).

DAY 25

1. Charles Carroll, *The Negro a Beast, or, In the Image of God* (Franklin Classics, 2018).
2. Baradaran, *Color of Money*, 10–11.

DAY 27

1. Ibram W. Kendi, *How to Be an Antiracist* (New York: One World, 2019), 13.
2. Kendi, 10.
3. Kendi, 13.

DAY 33

1. Carol Anderson, *White Rage: The Unspoken Truth of Our Racial Divide* (New York: Bloomsbury, 2016), 40–41.

DAY 36

1. Cleveland Jewish News, "Obama Administration Earmarks $12M for Holocaust Survivors," October 2, 2015. Accessed December 11, 2020. https://www.clevelandjewishnews.com/news/national_news/obama -administration-earmarks-m-for-holocaust-survivors/article_216db8a8 -6901-11e5-a3cb-1bdf0b03319f.html.

DAY 38

1. Robin DiAngelo, *White Fragility: Why It's So Hard for White People to Talk About Racism* (Boston: Beacon Press, 2018).

DAY 39

1. Frederick C. Van Tatenhove, *Ambition: Friend or Enemy* (Philadelphia: Westminster Press, 1984), 19.

APPENDIX

1. "Obama Administration Earmarks $12M for Holocaust Survivors," Jewish Telegraph Agency, October 1, 2015, https://www.jta.org/2015/10 /01/united-states/obama-administration-earmarks-12m-for-holocaust -survivors.
2. Erin Blakemore, "The Thorny History of Reparations in the United States," History.com, August 29, 2019, https://www.history.com/news /reparations-slavery-native-americans-japanese-internment.

CPSIA information can be obtained
at www.ICGtesting.com
Printed in the USA
LVHW090802010221
677389LV00025B/89

9 780664 266837